WORD ROOTS
A1

LEARNING THE BUILDING BLOCKS
OF BETTER SPELLING AND VOCABULARY

Word Roots Series
📖 Beginning 📖 A1 📖 A2 📖 B1 📖 B2
Flashcards: Beginning • A1 • A2 • B1

Written by
Cherie A. Plant

Graphic Design by
Annette Langenstein

Edited by
Patricia Gray
Alane Jennings

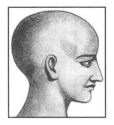

© 2012, 2002
THE CRITICAL THINKING CO.™
www.CriticalThinking.com
Phone: 800-458-4849 • Fax: 831-393-3277
P.O. Box 1610 • Seaside • CA 93955-1610
ISBN 978-0-89455-804-7

MIX
Paper from
responsible sources
FSC® C011935

The intellectual material in this product is the copyrighted property of The Critical Thinking Co.™ The individual or entity who initially purchased this product from The Critical Thinking Co.™ or one of its authorized resellers is licensed to reproduce (print or duplicate on paper) the activity pages in this product for use within one home or one classroom (maximum 35 students) each year. Our copyright and this limited reproduction permission (user) agreement strictly prohibit the sale of any of the copyrighted material in this product. Any reproduction beyond these expressed limits is strictly prohibited without the written permission of The Critical Thinking Co.™ Please visit http://www.criticalthinking.com/copyright for more information. The Critical Thinking Co.™ retains full intellectual property rights on all its products (eBooks, books, and software).
Printed in the United States of America by McNaughton & Gunn, Inc., Saline, MI (Sept. 2012)

TABLE OF CONTENTS

INTRODUCTION

"A mind is like a parachute; it works best when it is open."

—Lord Thomas Dewar

Word Roots is designed to help students expand their spelling, vocabulary, and comprehension skills. *Word Roots* is a uniquely designed and challenging workbook based on the word elements: roots, prefixes, and suffixes. Note that the roots used in this book originate from the Latin language—the foundation of much of our English language.

Roots, prefixes, and suffixes are the building blocks upon which all words are formed. A thorough knowledge of these elements will greatly enhance one's vocabulary and improve one's understanding of otherwise unfamiliar words. For example, understanding the meaning of the roots **struct**, **spect**, **frag**, **nov**, **manu**, and **script** would enable one to comprehend many words made from combinations of these elements, such as the following:

fragment	inscription	prospect
fragile	manuscript	manual
innovation	destruction	construct

A single Latin root can be the basis for many words in the English language. The significance of this lies in the fact that with every new root learned, the resulting growth of one's vocabulary can be truly astounding—and *Word Roots* provides the tools.

Definitions of Root, Prefix, and Suffix

A **root** is the element that gives the basic meaning of the word. In this book, the term root refers to the original Latin word. An English word may have two or more roots in it. Identifying these roots can help you to define a word you don't know.

A **prefix** is an element that is added to the beginning of a word. The prefix adds to or alters the meaning of the basic word. For example, the prefix **re-** means back, again. The root **tract** means to draw or pull.

> re + tract = retract means to draw or pull back

The prefix **con** means with or together.

> con + tract = contract means to draw together or shrink

A **suffix** is an element added to the end of a word. The suffix modifies the meaning of the base word. define the word grammatically, giving some indication as to the part of speech a word is.

Root: **dur** = harden, to last, lasting   Suffixes: **-able** (able to be), **-ation** (an action or process)

> dur + able = durable means having the quality of lasting

> dur + ation = duration means the length of time something lasts

Words such as <u>conven</u>tion and <u>digres</u>sion have both a prefix and a suffix joined to the root.

© 2012 The Critical Thinking Co.™ • www.CriticalThinking.com • 800-458-4849

How to Do the Activities

The worksheets help the student to meet several objectives. Given Latin elements and their definitions, the student will:

1. Identify these elements in English words.
2. Match each given word to its correct meaning.
3. Select the correct word to complete an unfinished sentence.

Identifying the Elements

The information below will help you identify the word elements (Objective 1 above).

- Words such as *act*, *tract*, *script*, and *herb* are both roots and words in and of themselves.

- A word can have more than one root, as shown below. Each root is circled.

$$manu + script \quad = \quad \text{(manu)(script)}$$

- In some words, connecting vowels and/or consonants are used to join word parts or to complete a word. For the sake of simplicity, connecting vowels and consonants used to join word parts or to complete words will appear in **gray**.

    herb + **i** + cide = herbicide
    fer + **t** + ile = fertile
    medi + **at** + or = mediator
    de + scrib**e** = describe

- In some cases, to help smooth the sound of the spoken word, a vowel is added to a root. This vowel (usually an **o**), is referred to as a <u>connecting vowel</u>, and the modified root is called a <u>combining form.</u> For example, the root **hydr** uses the connecting vowel **o** to produce the combining form **hydro,** which then combines with the root **electr** and the suffix **-ic** to form the word **hydroelectric**. In the lessons, an asterisk (*) is used to indicate if a root is a combining form.

    hydr + **o** = hydr**o** (combining form)
    hydr**o** + electr + ic = hydroelectric

Note: Some roots are considered to be combining forms, yet do not follow the general rule.

- The last letter of a root or suffix may be dropped when a suffix is added.

    mob + ile + ity   -ile drops the *e* in   mob<u>ility</u>

- Variations in spelling of roots are given when necessary. For example, **mob**, **mot**, or **mov** are all forms of the same Latin root. When more than one form is used, the root is listed with its alternatives, as shown below.

PREFIX	ROOT		SUFFIX
	mob/	move	
	mot/		
	mov		
	viv	live, life	

              © 2012 The Critical Thinking Co.™ • www.CriticalThinking.com • 800-458-4849

Completing the Exercises

Each worksheet has a 3-column box listing the word elements used on the page and their definitions. A prefix ends with a hyphen (-) indicating that text follows; a suffix begins with a hyphen indicating that text precedes it.

Focus Elements

Each worksheet is labeled at the top with a focus element(s) for that page. Every word in Column A uses at least one focus element. Non-focus element(s) used in the words in Column A are also shown in the prefix, root, or suffix list.

Have students do each worksheet as instructed below:

1. Study the meanings of the prefixes, roots, and suffixes given.

2. In Column A, identify the Latin elements used in each English word by circling the roots and underlining the prefixes and suffixes.

3. For each word in Column A, write the letter of the correct meaning from Column B.

4. Use the words from Column A to complete the sentences. Write the best word to complete each sentence.

PARTIAL SAMPLE WORKSHEET

FOCUS: mar					
PREFIX		**ROOT**		**SUFFIX**	
sub-	under	**aqua**	water	**-ine**	like, related to
		mar	sea		

DIRECTIONS: In Column A, identify the parts of each word by circling roots and then underlining prefixes and suffixes. Match each word to its correct meaning from Column B.

COLUMN A   **COLUMN B**

1. sub(mar)ine ____b____   a. blue-green in color, like sea water

2. (aqua)(mar)ine ____a____   b. being, living, or used under water

DIRECTIONS: Chose the word from Column A that best completes each sentence.

1. The bottom and sides of the swimming pool were painted __aquamarine__ .

2. The __submarine__ canyon in California's Monterey Bay is two miles deep.

Extension Worksheets

Extension activities, beginning on page 31, can be used for assessment or additional practice. Each group of exercises has three extension activities. Worksheets One, Two, and Three review pages 1–7; Worksheets Four, Five, and Six review pages 8–14; Worksheets Seven, Eight, and Nine review pages 15–22; and Worksheets Ten, Eleven, and Twelve review pages 23–30.

© 2012 The Critical Thinking Co.™ • www.CriticalThinking.com • 800-458-4849

PRETEST/POSTTEST

☞ Before starting *Word Roots*, test your existing knowledge of word meanings. On the blank spaces provided, write what you think the following words mean. However, do not score your answers at this time. After you complete the book, take the test again, and then score your answers. Compare your answers from before and after to determine the progress you've made.

1. traverse _____

2. regression _____

3. brevity _____

4. contradict _____

5. pugnacious _____

6. postscript _____

7. cumulative _____

8. accelerate _____

9. animate _____

10. emissary _____

11. loquacious _____

12. envision _____

13. vociferous _____

14. veracity _____

15. infraction _____

© 2012 The Critical Thinking Co.™ • www.CriticalThinking.com • 800-458-4849

STUDENT INTRODUCTION

Latin Word Parts

Latin roots, prefixes, and suffixes are the building blocks upon which many English words are formed.

A **root** is the part that gives the basic meaning of the word. Every word has a root.

> The root **frag** means break.
> **frag** + ment = fragment: a broken piece
> **frag** + ile = fragile: easily broken; delicate

A word can be formed from more than one root.

> The root **manu** means hand.
> The root **script** means write, written.
> **manu** + **script** = manuscript: a handwritten document

A **prefix** is a part that is added before the root. The prefix adds to or alters the meaning of the root. Not every word has a prefix.

> The prefix **de-** means from, away, down, apart; not.
> The root **struct** means build.
> **de** + struct = destruct: to take down

A word can have more than one prefix.

> The prefix **re-** means back, again.
> The prefix **con-** means with, together.
> The root **struct** means build.
> **re** + **con** + struct = reconstruct: to build again or put back together

A **suffix** is a part that is added to the end of the root. The suffix can define the English word grammatically or give a clue as to whether a word is a noun, verb, or adjective. Not every word has a suffix. Those that do can have more than one.

> The suffix **-ive** means tending to or performing.
> The suffix **-ate** means to make, to act; one who, that which.
> The suffix **-ity** means a state, quality, or act.
> The root **act** means to do, to drive.
> act + **ive** = active: engaged in action
>
> act + **ive** + **ate** = activate: to make active
>
> act + **ive** + **ity** = activity: state or quality of being active

Note: Some words may vary their spelling when combining roots or adding suffixes.

© 2012 The Critical Thinking Co.™ • www.CriticalThinking.com • 800-458-4849

Warm-Up Activity 1: Identifying Latin Word Parts

PREFIX	ROOT	SUFFIX
ac- con- in- inter- re-	aqua celer cept mar nomin nov tract vent	-al -ate -ice -ine -ion -tion

DIRECTIONS: Identify the Latin word parts used in the following English words. Circle the Latin root and then underline the prefixes and suffixes.

1. in(nov)ate

2. contraction

3. convention

4. intercept

5. nominate

6. retract

7. accelerate

8. aquamarine

9. nominal

10. novice

© 2012 The Critical Thinking Co.™ • www.CriticalThinking.com • 800-458-4849

Warm-Up Activity 2: Prefixes

PREFIXES			
con-	with, together	**ob-**	to, toward, against
counter-	against, opposite	**pro-**	for, before, forward
di-	apart, away; not	**re-**	back, again
inter-	between, among		

DIRECTIONS: Choose one or more prefixes from the box to complete a word that matches the definition given on the right. Write the prefix and completed word on the lines.

	Prefix		Root		Word	
1.	inter	+	act (to do, to drive)	=	interact	to do things or talk with others
2.	_____	+	act (to do, to drive)	=	_____	to act directly against; to prevent from affecting
3.	_____	+	act (to do, to drive)	=	_____	to respond to something (by an action or show of feelings)
4.	_____	+	gress (step)	=	_____	a movement forward or onward; improvement
5.	_____	+	gress (step)	=	_____	to move away from
6.	_____	+	struct (build)	=	_____	to act against something being built or completed
7.	_____	+	struct (build)	=	_____	to form by putting together parts
8.	_____ + _____	+	struct (build)	=	_____	to put something back together

Warm-Up Activity 3: Suffixes

<table>
<tr><th colspan="2" align="center">SUFFIXES</th></tr>
<tr><td>**-able** able to be</td><td>**-ile** like, of, relating to</td></tr>
<tr><td>**-al** like, related to; an action or process</td><td>**-ion** an action or process; state, quality, act</td></tr>
<tr><td rowspan="2"></td><td>**-ity** state, quality, act</td></tr>
<tr><td>**-ous** having the quality of</td></tr>
<tr><td>**-ary** that which, someone or something that belongs to; of, related to; one who</td><td>**-y** state of, quality, act; body, group</td></tr>
</table>

DIRECTIONS: Choose one or more suffixes from the box to complete a word that matches the definition given on the right. Write the suffix and completed word on the lines.

	Root		Suffix	Word	
1.	lumin (light)	+	_ous_	=	luminous — giving off or reflecting light
2.	lumin (light)	+	_____	=	_____ an object, like a star, that gives off light; a famous person (a "star")
3.	memor (remember)	+	_____	=	_____ an ability to retain knowledge; an individual's stock of retained knowledge
4.	memor (remember)	+	_____	=	_____ easy to be remembered
5.	memori (remember)	+	_____	=	_____ related to remembering a person or event
6.	mob (move)	+	_____ + _____	=	_____ relating to the quality of being able to move
7.	mot (move)	+	_____	=	_____ the act or process of moving
8.	mov (move)	+	_____	=	_____ able to move or be moved easily

© 2012 The Critical Thinking Co.™ • www.CriticalThinking.com • 800-458-4849

Warm-Up Activity 4: Thinking About Meaning

DIRECTIONS: Use the meaning of the word parts to define each of the following words. The first has been done for you.

1. **construct** = con + struct
    con- means with, together; **struct** means build

    Then *construct* means _____ to form by putting together parts. _____

2. **marine** = mar + ine
    mar means sea; **-ine** means like, related to

    Then *marine* means _____

3. **fragile** = frag + ile
    frag means break; **-ile** means like, of, relating to

    Then *fragile* means _____

4. **incredible** = in + cred + ible
    in- means in, into; not; **cred** means believe; **-ible** means able to be

    Then *incredible* means _____

5. **decelerate** = de + celer + ate
    de- means from, away, down, apart; not; **celer** means fast; **-ate** means to make, to act; one who, that which

    Then *decelerate* means _____

6. **interrupt** = inter + rupt
    inter- means between, among; **rupt** means break, burst

    Then *interrupt* means _____

7. **conclusion** = con + clus + ion
    con- means with, together; **clus** means close; **-ion** means an action or process; state, quality, act

    Then *conclusion* means _____

8. **carnivorous** = carni + vor + ous
    carni means flesh, meat; **vor** means eat; **-ous** means having the quality of

    Then *carnivorous* means _____

© 2012 The Critical Thinking Co.™ • www.CriticalThinking.com • 800-458-4849

FOCUS: struct

PREFIX		ROOT	SUFFIX	
con-	with, together	**struct** build	**-ion**	an action or process; state, quality act
de-	from, away, down, apart; not		**-ure**	state, quality, act; that which; process, condition
infra-	beneath			
ob-	to, toward, against			
re-	back, again			

DIRECTIONS: In Column A, identify the parts of each word by circling roots and then underlining prefixes and suffixes. Match each word to its correct meaning from Column B.

COLUMN A

1. con(struct) _____
2. destruction _____
3. infrastructure _____
4. obstruction _____
5. reconstruction _____

COLUMN B

a. the act of destroying; a state of damage
b. to form by putting together parts
c. the act of putting back together
d. underlying framework of a system
e. an obstacle or something put up against something else

DIRECTIONS: Choose the best word from Column A for each sentence. Use each word only once.

1. The hurricane that struck the Florida coast caused a great deal of

   _____.

2. The accident on the highway was a major _____ to the flow of traffic.

3. Jeremy kept busy all afternoon with the _____ of his Lego tower from the fallen pieces.

4. The _____ of a school consists of teachers, administration, and a school board.

5. He was hoping to _____ the new model airplane within a week.

© 2012 The Critical Thinking Co.™ • www.CriticalThinking.com • 800-458-4849

FOCUS: tract, vinc/vince

PREFIX		ROOT		SUFFIX	
con-	with, together	tract	to draw or pull, drag, draw out	-ible	able to be
ex-	out, away, from	vinc/	conquer	-ion	an action or process; state, quality, act
in-	in, into; not	vince			
re-	back, again				

DIRECTIONS: In Column A, identify the parts of each word by circling roots and then underlining prefixes and suffixes. Match each word to its correct meaning from Column B.

COLUMN A

1. con(tract)ion _____
2. extraction _____
3. retract _____
4. convince _____
5. invincible _____

COLUMN B

a. unbeatable; impossible to overcome
b. to persuade by argument or evidence
c. act of drawing together or shrinking
d. process of withdrawing, pulling out
e. to draw or pull back

DIRECTIONS: Choose the best word from Column A for each sentence. Use each word only once.

1. Bridges must be built to withstand the expansion and _____ caused by weather.

2. The attorney tried to _____ the jury that the defendant was not guilty.

3. The tooth _____ was done by an oral surgeon.

4. The brave troops were trained to march forth as though they were

   _____.

5. Cindy wished she could _____ what she said, but her friends had already heard it.

© 2012 The Critical Thinking Co.™ • www.CriticalThinking.com • 800-458-4849

FOCUS: mob/mot/mov

PREFIX		ROOT		SUFFIX	
com-	with, together	**mob/**	move	**-able**	able to be
im-	in, into; not	**mot/**		**-ile**	like, of, relating to
pro-	for, before, forward	**mov**		**-ion**	an action or process; state, quality, act
re-	back, again			**il-ity**	state, quality, act

DIRECTIONS: In Column A, identify the parts of each word by circling roots and then underlining prefixes and suffixes. Match each word to its correct meaning from Column B.

COLUMN A

1. com(mo)ion _____
2. immobile _____
3. mobility _____
4. promotion _____
5. removable _____

COLUMN B

a. an advancement in rank or position
b. relating to the quality of being able to move
c. able to be taken or carried away
d. the scene of noisy confusion or activity
e. motionless; unable to move

DIRECTIONS: Choose the best word from Column A for each sentence. Use each word only once.

1. She woke up in the middle of the night because of the _____ outside the tent.

2. His _____ was due to his commitment to his work.

3. The winter coat has a _____ lining that zips out.

4. The cat would have more _____ outside the cage.

5. The _____ locomotive was in need of repair.

© 2012 The Critical Thinking Co.™ • www.CriticalThinking.com • 800-458-4849

FOCUS: brev, cede/ceed/cess

	PREFIX		ROOT		SUFFIX
ab-	away, from	**brev**	short	**i-ate**	to make, to act; one who, that which
ac-	to, toward, near	**cede/**	go, yield	**-ible**	able to be
pro-	for, before, forward	**ceed/**		**-ity**	state, quality, act
se-	apart, aside	**cess**			

DIRECTIONS: In Column A, identify the parts of each word by circling roots and then underlining prefixes and suffixes. Match each word to its correct meaning from Column B.

COLUMN A

1. a_b(brev)iate_ _____
2. b r e v i t y _____
3. a c c e s s i b l e _____
4. p r o c e e d _____
5. s e c e d e _____

COLUMN B

a. quality of being brief; shortness in time
b. to formally break away from
c. easily entered, approached, or obtained
d. to shorten
e. to go forward, especially after stopping

DIRECTIONS: Choose the best word from Column A for each sentence. Use each word only once.

1. The neighborhood was unhappy with the government and attempted to

   _____ from the city.

2. The ice skaters were warned to _____ with caution on the rough ice rink.

3. The audience was tired and appreciated the _____ of the politician's speech.

4. The students learned how to _____ the state names.

5. The cookie jar was on the kitchen counter and not on a high shelf, so the children found it easily _____.

                © 2012 The Critical Thinking Co.™ • www.CriticalThinking.com • 800-458-4849

FOCUS: celer, gress

	PREFIX	ROOT		SUFFIX	
ac-	to, toward, near	**celer**	fast	**-ate**	to make, to act; one who, that which
de-	from, away, down, apart; not	**gress**	step	**-ion**	an action or process; state, quality, act
di-	apart, away; not				
pro-	for, before, forward				
re-	back, again				

DIRECTIONS: In Column A, identify the parts of each word by circling roots and then underlining prefixes and suffixes. Match each word to its correct meaning from Column B.

COLUMN A

1. a<u>c</u>(cele)<u>r</u>ate _____
2. decelerate _____
3. digression _____
4. progress _____
5. regression _____

COLUMN B

a. to reduce the speed of

b. a departure from the main issue, subject, etc.

c. a movement forward or onward; improvement

d. a movement backward to an earlier state

e. to increase the speed of

DIRECTIONS: Choose the best word from Column A for each sentence. Use each word only once.

1. As the car approached the icy curve, the driver needed to _____.

2. The student's _____ from the book topic annoyed the teacher.

3. The contractor was hoping to _____ the building process so the office complex would be finished before winter started.

4. The teacher was happy to see the _____ his class had made in learning multiplication.

5. The illness had caused a gradual _____ in his ability to speak.

© 2012 The Critical Thinking Co.™ • www.CriticalThinking.com • 800-458-4849   5

FOCUS: avi/avia, memor

PREFIX	ROOT	SUFFIX	
com- with, together	**avi/** bird **avia** **memor** remember	**i-al**	like, related to; an action or process
		-ary	that which; someone or something that belongs to; of, related to; one who
		-ate	to make, to act; one who, that which
		-trix	feminine
		-y	state of, quality, act; body, group

DIRECTIONS: In Column A, identify the parts of each word by circling roots and then underlining prefixes and suffixes. Match each word to its correct meaning from Column B.

COLUMN A	COLUMN B
1. (avi)ary _____	a. related to remembering a person or event
2. aviatrix _____	b. a large enclosure in which birds are kept
3. commemorate _____	c. a woman airplane pilot
4. memory _____	d. to honor the memory of, as by a ceremony
5. memorial _____	e. an ability to retain knowledge; an individual's stock of retained knowledge

DIRECTIONS: Choose the best word from Column A for each sentence. Use each word only once.

1. The highlight of their trip to the zoo was visiting the _____.

2. The veterans of World War II gathered together to _____ those who had died.

3. The _____ performed some of the most daring feats we had ever seen.

4. His head injury caused a partial loss of _____ that lasted for weeks.

5. The families held a _____ service for their grandfather who recently passed away.

© 2012 The Critical Thinking Co.™ • www.CriticalThinking.com • 800-458-4849

FOCUS: mar, pugn

PREFIX		ROOT		SUFFIX	
re-	back, again	**aqua**	water	**-acious**	having the quality of
sub-	under, below	**mar**	sea	**-ant**	one who, that which; state, quality
		pugn	fight	**-ine**	like, related to

DIRECTIONS: In Column A, identify the parts of each word by circling roots and then underlining prefixes and suffixes. Match each word to its correct meaning from Column B.

COLUMN A

1. aquamarine _____
2. marine _____
3. submarine _____
4. pugnacious _____
5. repugnant _____

COLUMN B

a. distasteful; offensive or revolting
b. having a quarrelsome or aggressive nature
c. blue-green in color, like sea water
d. being, living or used under water
e. of or pertaining to the sea

DIRECTIONS: Choose the best word from Column A for each sentence. Use each word only once.

1. The woman grew up near the ocean and decided to pursue a career in

_____ biology.

2. The man's _____ behavior resulted in his hitting someone.

3. The _____ canyon in California's Monterey Bay is two miles deep.

4. Spitting in public is _____.

5. The bottom and sides of the swimming pool were painted _____ .

© 2012 The Critical Thinking Co.™ • www.CriticalThinking.com • 800-458-4849

FOCUS: act, aud

PREFIX		ROOT		SUFFIX	
counter-	against, opposite	**act**	to do, to drive	**i-ence**	state, quality, act
in-	in, into; not	**aud**	hear	**-ible**	able to be
inter-	between, among			**-ion**	an action or process; state, quality, act
re-	back, again				

DIRECTIONS: In Column A, identify the parts of each word by circling roots and then underlining prefixes and suffixes. Match each word to its correct meaning from Column B.

COLUMN A		COLUMN B
1. counter(act) _____		a. communication between two or more things
2. interaction _____		b. to act directly against; to prevent from affecting
3. reaction _____		c. a group of listeners or spectators
4. audience _____		d. a response
5. inaudible _____		e. unable to be heard

DIRECTIONS: Choose the best word from Column A for each sentence. Use each word only once.

1. Her _____ to the surprise birthday party was one of shock.

2. There was a great deal of positive _____ among the classmates.

3. Comedians perform best with a live _____ .

4. The doctor advised his patient to drink plenty of liquids to _____ the dehydrating effects of the medication.

5. The children were talking so quietly that they were almost _____ .

© 2012 The Critical Thinking Co.™ • www.CriticalThinking.com • 800-458-4849

FOCUS: juven, vene/vent

PREFIX		ROOT		SUFFIX	
circum-	around	**juven**	young	**-ate**	to make, to act; one who, that which
con-	with, together	**vene/**	come	**-ile**	like, of, relating to
inter-	between, among	**vent**		**-ion**	an action or process; state, quality, act
re-	back, again				

DIRECTIONS: In Column A, identify the parts of each word by circling roots and then underlining prefixes and suffixes. Match each word to its correct meaning from Column B.

COLUMN A

1. juvenile _____
2. rejuvenate _____
3. circumvent _____
4. convention _____
5. intervene _____

COLUMN B

a. to come between; to intercede
b. youthful or childish; immature
c. to go around; to bypass restrictions
d. to bring back to youthful strength or appearance
e. a gathering or assembly of people with a common interest

DIRECTIONS: Choose the best word from Column A for each sentence. Use each word only once.

1. The student attempted to _____ the no-hats rule at school by wearing a sun visor.

2. The bus driver was forced to _____ when two passengers began shouting at each other.

3. The aging beauty queen was hopeful that cosmetic surgery would _____ her looks.

4. The mother thought her teen daughter's temper tantrum in public showed _____ behavior.

5. Scientists from all over the world attended the annual _____.

FOCUS: cogn, termin

PREFIX		ROOT		SUFFIX	
de-	from, away, down, apart; not	**cogn**	know	**-al**	like, related to; an action or process
		termin	end, limit	**-ate**	to make, to act; one who, that which
ex-	out, away, from			**-ation**	an action or process
re-	back, again			**-ize**	to make, to act
				i-tion	state, quality, act

DIRECTIONS: In Column A, identify the parts of each word by circling roots and then underlining prefixes and suffixes. Match each word to its correct meaning from Column B.

COLUMN A

1. (cogn)ition _____
2. recognize _____
3. determination _____
4. exterminate _____
5. terminal _____

COLUMN B

a. to identify someone or something seen before

b. process of acquiring knowledge

c. to destroy or get rid of completely

d. an intent to reach a goal

e. related to something leading to the end or to death

DIRECTIONS: Choose the best word from Column A for each sentence. Use each word only once.

1. The child recovered from the illness the doctors had said was _____.

2. Dan's _____ to win every race got him to the Olympics.

3. Since they hadn't seen each other in many years, the former classmates failed to _____ each other.

4. I called a pest control company to _____ the fleas in our house.

5. Scientists have studied the brains of infants and their _____.

© 2012 The Critical Thinking Co.™ • www.CriticalThinking.com • 800-458-4849

FOCUS: scribe/script

PREFIX		ROOT	SUFFIX	
circum-	around	**scribe/** write, written	**-ion**	an action or process; state, quality, act
de-	from, away, down, apart; not	**script**		
in-	in, into; not			
post-	after			
pre-	before, in front of			

DIRECTIONS: In Column A, identify the parts of each word by circling roots and then underlining prefixes and suffixes. Match each word to its correct meaning from Column B.

COLUMN A

1. circum(scribe) _____
2. describe _____
3. inscription _____
4. postscript _____
5. prescription _____

COLUMN B

a. to represent with words or pictures

b. a written order for medicine

c. an engraving on a coin or other object

d. to draw around; to encircle

e. an addition to an already completed letter, article, or book

DIRECTIONS: Choose the best word from Column A for each sentence. Use each word only once.

1. She squeezed in a _____ at the bottom of her letter telling the date of her return.

2. The math class was learning to _____ various geometric figures with a compass.

3. The _____ on the medallion showed the date of her birthday.

4. The nurse called the pharmacy with the _____ for the patient's medicine.

5. She asked me to _____ a sea otter because she had never seen one.

FOCUS: cap, cept, tact

PREFIX		ROOT		SUFFIX	
con-	with, together	capt/	take, hold	-ile	like, of, relating to
in-	in, into; not	cept		-ure	state, quality, act, that which; process, condition
inter-	between, among	tact	touch		
re-	back, again				

DIRECTIONS: In Column A, identify the parts of each word by circling roots and then underlining prefixes and suffixes. Match each word to its correct meaning from Column B.

COLUMN A   **COLUMN B**

1. inter(cept) _____   a. the state of touching or meeting

2. recapture _____   b. of or relating to the sense of touch

3. contact _____   c. to stop or interrupt the course of

4. intact _____   d. the taking back of something

5. tactile _____   e. with nothing missing; left whole

DIRECTIONS: Choose the best word from Column A for each sentence. Use each word only once.

1. The package arrived torn, but the things inside were _____.

2. The authorities were pleased to announce the _____ of the escaped prisoners.

3. The soccer player was trying to _____ a forward pass.

4. On _____, the wallpaper stuck to the wall.

5. A blind person uses _____ objects to learn what something looks like.

                © 2012 The Critical Thinking Co.™ • www.CriticalThinking.com • 800-458-4849

FOCUS: dict, rupt

PREFIX		ROOT		SUFFIX	
contra-	against, opposite	**dict**	say, speak	**-ion**	an action or process; state, quality, act
cor-	with, together	**rupt**	break, burst		
inter-	between, among			**-ure**	state, quality, act; that which; process, condition
pre-	before, in front of				

DIRECTIONS: In Column A, identify the parts of each word by circling roots and then underlining prefixes and suffixes. Match each word to its correct meaning from Column B.

COLUMN A

1. <u>contra</u>(dict) _____
2. prediction _____
3. corruption _____
4. interrupt _____
5. rupture _____

COLUMN B

a. to stop or hinder by breaking in on
b. to express or imply the opposite of
c. a breaking apart or the state of being broken apart
d. a statement foretelling the future
e. a break with what is legally or morally right

DIRECTIONS: Choose the best word from Column A for each sentence. Use each word only once.

1. His angry facial expressions _____ his friendly words.

2. The promise of quick wealth led to widespread _____ in the city government.

3. An earthquake caused the _____ of the underground pipe.

4. She made a _____ that her candidate would win the election.

5. The referee was forced to _____ the soccer game because of a sudden hailstorm.

© 2012 The Critical Thinking Co.™ • www.CriticalThinking.com • 800-458-4849

FOCUS: pose/posit

	PREFIX	ROOT	SUFFIX	
com-	with, together	**pose/** place, put	**-ion**	an action or process; state, quality, act
de-	from, away, down, apart; not	**posit**		
ex-	out, away, from			
im-	in, into; not			
op-	to, toward, against			

DIRECTIONS: In Column A, identify the parts of each word by circling roots and then underlining prefixes and suffixes. Match each word to its correct meaning from Column B.

COLUMN A

1. ex(pose) _____
2. composition _____
3. deposit _____
4. imposition _____
5. opposition _____

COLUMN B

a. an excessive or unjust burden placed on someone

b. to put down or in a safe place

c. an arrangement or putting together of parts

d. the act of resistance or action against

e. to place something where it can be seen; to put in an unprotected situation

DIRECTIONS: Choose the best word from Column A for each sentence. Use each word only once.

1. She lifted the garbage can lid to _____ the trash within.

2. The candidate faced strong _____ to his program.

3. The storm is expected to _____ twenty inches of snow.

4. She won first place for her musical _____.

5. He felt that asking his neighbor to take him to work was too much of an

   _____.

          © 2012 The Critical Thinking Co.™ • www.CriticalThinking.com • 800-458-4849

FOCUS: fract/frag

PREFIX	ROOT	SUFFIX	
in- in, into; not	**fract/** break **frag**	**-ile**	like, of, relating to
		-ion	an action or process; state, quality, act
		-ment	that which, state, quality, act
		-ure	state, quality, act; that which; process, condition

DIRECTIONS: In Column A, identify the parts of each word by circling roots and then underlining prefixes and suffixes. Match each word to its correct meaning from Column B.

COLUMN A

1. fraction _____
2. fracture _____
3. infraction _____
4. fragile _____
5. fragment _____

COLUMN B

a. a broken piece

b. the act of breaking the limits or rules

c. easily broken; delicate

d. a part or element of a larger whole

e. a break, crack, or split

DIRECTIONS: Choose the best word from Column A for each sentence. Use each word only once.

1. The once popular toy was no longer in demand and was selling at a

   _____ of its former price.

2. They recovered only one large _____ of the beautiful vase after it fell.

3. The crystal bowl was extremely _____.

4. Chewing gum in school is an _____ of school policy.

5. The bone _____ was clearly visible on the x-ray.

FOCUS: anim, cred

PREFIX		ROOT		SUFFIX	
in-	in, into; not	**anim**	spirit, life	**-ate**	to make, to act; one who, that which
		cred	believe	**-ence**	state, quality, act
		equ	equal, fair	**-ible**	able to be
				-ity	state, quality, act
				-ulous	having the quality of

DIRECTIONS: In Column A, identify the parts of each word by circling roots and then underlining prefixes and suffixes. Match each word to its correct meaning from Column B.

COLUMN A

1. (anim)ate _____
2. equanimity _____
3. credence _____
4. incredible _____
5. incredulous _____

COLUMN B

a. to give spirit, life, motion, or activity to

b. too extraordinary and impossible to believe

c. disbelieving; not believing

d. calm temperament; evenness of temper

e. belief; acceptance as true or valid

DIRECTIONS: Choose the best word from Column A for each sentence. Use each word only once.

1. The tightrope walker performed the most _____ balancing act we had ever seen.

2. The student's excuse for tardiness received an _____ look from the teacher.

3. His _____ was apparent even when things got stressful.

4. The eyewitness gave _____ to the suspect's story.

5. The clown's visit to the children's hospital helped _____ the young patients.

© 2012 The Critical Thinking Co.™ • www.CriticalThinking.com • 800-458-4849

FOCUS: duct, vol

PREFIX		ROOT		SUFFIX	
ab-	away, from	**duct**	lead	**-ent**	one who, that which; like, related to
bene-	good, well	**vol**	will, wish	**-ion**	an action or process; state, quality, act
de-	from, away, down, apart; not			**i-tion**	state, quality, act
in-	in, into; not				

DIRECTIONS: In Column A, identify the parts of each word by circling roots and then underlining prefixes and suffixes. Match each word to its correct meaning from Column B.

COLUMN A

1. a b d u c t i o n _____
2. d e d u c t i o n _____
3. i n d u c t _____
4. b e n e v o l e n t _____
5. v o l i t i o n _____

COLUMN B

a. to formally install someone to an office or position
b. a taking away by force
c. showing kindness or goodwill
d. a subtraction of an amount
e. the act of making a choice or a decision

DIRECTIONS: Choose the best word from Column A for each sentence. Use each word only once.

1. The waiter made a _____ from the bill to make up for the customers' long wait for their food to arrive.

2. On Wednesday, the board members will _____ the new officers.

3. In Greek mythology, the _____ of Helen from Sparta began the Trojan War.

4. The _____ doctor volunteered his services to the homeless.

5. She joined the Peace Corps of her own _____.

© 2012 The Critical Thinking Co.™ • www.CriticalThinking.com • 800-458-4849

FOCUS: vers/verse/vert

PREFIX		ROOT		SUFFIX	
a-	away, from; not, without	**vers/**	turn	**-ion**	an action or process; state, quality, act
con-	with, together	**verse/**			
intro-	within	**vert**			
tra-	across, through				

DIRECTIONS: In Column A, identify the parts of each word by circling roots and then underlining prefixes and suffixes. Match each word to its correct meaning from Column B.

COLUMN A   **COLUMN B**

1. a<u>vers</u>ion _____   a. to move across or turn back and forth across

2. convert _____   b. an outgoing person

3. extrovert _____   c. turning inward; focusing on oneself

4. introversion _____   d. to turn into or transform

5. traverse _____   e. the act of turning away from; a dislike of something

DIRECTIONS: Choose the best word from Column A for each sentence. Use each word only once.

1. Native American tribes would _____ the plains in search of buffalo.

2. The child _____ grew up to be a famous comedian.

3. Vegetarians have an _____ to eating meat.

4. He planned to _____ the garage into another bedroom.

5. He believed his _____ came from being an only child.

© 2012 The Critical Thinking Co.™ • www.CriticalThinking.com • 800-458-4849

FOCUS: loqu, nom/nomin

PREFIX		ROOT		SUFFIX	
e-	out, away, from	loqu	speak	-acious	having the quality of
mis-	bad, wrong	nom/	name, law, custom,	-al	like, related to; an action or process
		nomin	order	-ate	to make, to act; one who, that which
				-ent	one who, that which; like, related to
				-er	one who, that which

DIRECTIONS: In Column A, identify the parts of each word by circling roots and then underlining prefixes and suffixes. Match each word to its correct meaning from Column B.

COLUMN A

1. e(loqu)ent _____
2. loquacious _____
3. nominal _____
4. nominate _____
5. misnomer _____

COLUMN B

a. very talkative

b. an error in naming a person or thing

c. being something in name only but not in reality

d. to name for election or appointment; to designate

e. speaking beautifully and forcefully

DIRECTIONS: Choose the best word from Column A for each sentence. Use each word only once.

1. The students were asked to _____ three classmates for president.

2. The teacher corrected the student's _____ in his report.

3. Until the official election, he was designated the _____ leader.

4. The young princess impressed people with her _____ address to the peace organization.

5. The new neighbors proved to be friendly and _____.

© 2012 The Critical Thinking Co.™ • www.CriticalThinking.com • 800-458-4849

FOCUS: manu, vor/vour

	PREFIX		ROOT		SUFFIX
de-	from, away, down, apart; not	**carni**	flesh, meat	**-acious**	having the quality of
		manu	hand	**-al**	like, related to; an action or process
		script	write, written		
		vor/ vour	eat	**-ous**	having the quality of

DIRECTIONS: In Column A, identify the parts of each word by circling roots and then underlining prefixes and suffixes. Match each word to its correct meaning from Column B.

COLUMN A   COLUMN B

1. (man)al _____   a. flesh-eating

2. manuscript _____   b. desiring or eating food in great quantities

3. carnivorous _____   c. having to do with the hands

4. devour _____   d. to eat quickly

5. voracious _____   e. a handwritten document or author's original text

DIRECTIONS: Choose the best word from Column A for each sentence. Use each word only once.

1. After being stranded in the wilderness for three days, she had a _____ appetite.

2. He liked his job as a landscaper because it involved _____ labor and being outside.

3. Other dinosaurs were not afraid of being attacked by the brontosaurus because it was not _____.

4. My dog will _____ her food as soon as the dish hits the floor.

5. Reading an ancient _____ can reveal information about a culture that no longer exists.

© 2012 The Critical Thinking Co.™ • www.CriticalThinking.com • 800-458-4849

FOCUS: enni, later

PREFIX		ROOT		SUFFIX	
bi-	two	**enni**	year	**-al**	like, related to; an action or process
cent-	hundred	**later**	side		
per-	through, very				
uni-	one				

DIRECTIONS: In Column A, identify the parts of each word by circling roots and then underlining prefixes and suffixes. Match each word to its correct meaning from Column B.

COLUMN A

1. <u>bi</u> <u>cent</u>(enn)<u>al</u> _____
2. centennial _____
3. perennial _____
4. bilateral _____
5. unilateral _____

COLUMN B

a. affecting one side of something

b. of or relating to an age or period of 200 years

c. of or involving two sides; reciprocal

d. of or relating to an age or period of 100 years

e. lasting through many years

DIRECTIONS: Choose the best word from Column A for each sentence. Use each word only once.

1. Each spring the _____ flowers she planted during her first year at the house bloom again.

2. In 1976, the United States had its _____ anniversary.

3. The US and Mexico benefit from a _____ trade agreement.

4. The country made a _____ decision to stop selling arms.

5. The _____ celebration honored the author John Steinbeck, who was born in the early 1900s.

© 2012 The Critical Thinking Co.™ • www.CriticalThinking.com • 800-458-4849

FOCUS: tempor, ver

PREFIX		ROOT		SUFFIX	
con-	with, together	**tempor**	time	**-acity**	the quality of
ex-	out, away, from	**ver**	truth	**-aneous**	having the quality of
				-ary	that which; someone or something that belongs to; of, related to; one who
				i-fy	to make, to act, to do

DIRECTIONS: In Column A, identify the parts of each word by circling roots and then underlining prefixes and suffixes. Match each word to its correct meaning from Column B.

COLUMN A

1. con(tempor)ary _____
2. extemporaneous_____
3. temporary _____
4. veracity _____
5. verify _____

COLUMN B

a. lasting for a limited time

b. of the same time; modern time

c. to confirm; to prove to be true

d. done without any preparation; impromptu

e. truth; honesty

DIRECTIONS: Choose the best word from Column A for each sentence. Use each word only once.

1. The mayor was known for his _____ speaking ability.

2. Although the mother was upset with her son, she praised him for his

   _____ after he admitted to eating all of the candy.

3. They called the store to _____ the winning lotto numbers.

4. Bad weather caused a _____ delay in their plans.

5. He enjoyed both _____ and classical music.

                    © 2012 The Critical Thinking Co.™ • www.CriticalThinking.com • 800-458-4849

FOCUS: dur, viv

PREFIX	ROOT	SUFFIX	
re- back, again	**dur** harden, to last, lasting **viv** live, life	**-able** **-acious** **-al** **-ation** **-id**	able to be having the quality of like, related to; an action or process an action or process like, related to

DIRECTIONS: In Column A, identify the parts of each word by circling roots and then underlining prefixes and suffixes. Match each word to its correct meaning from Column B.

COLUMN A

1. dur̲a̲b̲l̲e̲   _____
2. d u r a t i o n   _____
3. r e v i v a l   _____
4. v i v a c i o u s _____
5. v i v i d   _____

COLUMN B

a. lively in appearance; bright; intense; strong
b. high-spirited and full of life
c. the length of time something lasts
d. the act of bringing back to life; renewed interest in
e. having the quality of lasting

DIRECTIONS: Choose the best word from Column A for each sentence. Use each word only once.

1. The artist's use of _____ shapes and colors made his work very appealing.

2. The actress was loved by all because of her _____ personality.

3. Her hiccups lasted the _____ of the lunch hour.

4. The _____ of the Broadway play proved to be a box office hit.

5. Denim is known for its _____ nature.

FOCUS: claim/clam, equ/equi

PREFIX		ROOT		SUFFIX	
ex-	out, away, from	**claim/ clam**	call out, shout	**-ate**	to make, to act; one who, that which
pro-	for, before, forward	**equ/ equi***	equal, fair	**-ation**	an action or process
		voc	voice, call	**-ity**	state, quality, act

DIRECTIONS: In Column A, identify the parts of each word by circling roots and then underlining prefixes and suffixes. Match each word to its correct meaning from Column B.

COLUMN A

1. ex(claim) _____
2. proclamation _____
3. equation _____
4. equity _____
5. equivocate _____

COLUMN B

a. fairness; the state of being just or fair

b. a statement of equality

c. something announced officially in public

d. to cry out or speak in a strong or sudden manner

e. to use misleading language that could be interpreted in different ways

DIRECTIONS: Choose the best word from Column A for each sentence. Use each word only once.

1. The skaters complained about the lack of _____ in the judges' decision.

2. The king issued a _____ that all foreign prisoners would be released and returned to their home countries.

3. Jean was a shy child who surprised her classmates when she jumped up to

   _____ that she thought the rules of the game were not fair.

4. The _____ showed that two apples weighed the same as one melon.

5. The boss no longer believed the employee because he continued to

   _____ about why he was late.

*For more information, please see the Introduction.

 © 2012 The Critical Thinking Co.™ • www.CriticalThinking.com • 800-458-4849

FOCUS: cumul, lumin

PREFIX		ROOT		SUFFIX	
ac-	to, toward, near	**cumul**	mass, heap	**-ary**	that which; someone or something that belongs to; of, related to; one who
il-	in, into; not	**lumin**	light	**-ate**	to make, to act; one who, that which
				at-ive	tending to or performing
				-ous	having the quality of

DIRECTIONS: In Column A, identify the parts of each word by circling roots and then underlining prefixes and suffixes. Match each word to its correct meaning from Column B.

COLUMN A

1. ac(cumul)ate _____
2. cumulative _____
3. illuminate _____
4. luminary _____
5. luminous _____

COLUMN B

a. gradually building up
b. to give light to
c. to gather or pile up little by little
d. giving off or reflecting light
e. an object, like a star, that gives off light; a famous person ("star")

DIRECTIONS: Choose the best word from Column A for each sentence. Use each word only once.

1. The _____ stars shone brightly in the dark of night.

2. Her scrapbook was a _____ project that took many years to complete.

3. The winner of the game had to _____ the most points.

4. The fans at the famous Hollywood restaurant kept watch for a glimpse of their favorite _____.

5. They installed spotlights in order to _____ the building.

FOCUS: nov, voc/voci

PREFIX		ROOT		SUFFIX	
in-	in, into; not	nov	new	-able	able to be
re-	back, again	voc/ voci	voice, call	-ate	to make, to act; one who, that which
				-ation	an action or process
				-ferous	producing
				-ice	one who, that which

DIRECTIONS: In Column A, identify the parts of each word by circling roots and then underlining prefixes and suffixes. Match each word to its correct meaning from Column B.

COLUMN A

1. in(nov)ation _____
2. novice _____
3. renovate _____
4. revocable _____
5. vociferous _____

COLUMN B

a. to make something like new again
b. loud, noisy
c. the act or process of inventing something new
d. a person who is new to an activity; a beginner
e. able to be repealed or withdrawn

DIRECTIONS: Choose the best word from Column A for each sentence. Use each word only once.

1. The new coach's contract was _____ if he was unable to improve the team.

2. Owners of very old homes often _____ them so they look exactly as they did when they were first built.

3. Making items from plastic was an _____ of the 20th century.

4. The team was _____ when the umpire called their batter out.

5. Everyone could see he was a _____ when he repeatedly fell off the skateboard.

© 2012 The Critical Thinking Co.™ • www.CriticalThinking.com • 800-458-4849

FOCUS: clude/clus, herbi

PREFIX		ROOT		SUFFIX	
con-	with, together	**clude/**	close	**-cide**	kill
ex-	out, away, from	**clus**		**-ion**	an action or process; state, quality, act
se-	apart, aside	**herbi**	grass	**-ous**	having the quality of
		vor	eat		

DIRECTIONS: In Column A, identify the parts of each word by circling roots and then underlining prefixes and suffixes. Match each word to its correct meaning from Column B.

COLUMN A   **COLUMN B**

1. <u>con</u>(clus)<u>ion</u>   _____   a. plant-eating

2. exclusion   _____   b. the end or last part

3. seclude   _____   c. to keep away from; to isolate

4. herbicide   _____   d. a shutting out; rejection

5. herbivorous   _____   e. any chemical used to kill unwanted plants, etc.

DIRECTIONS: Choose the best word from Column A for each sentence. Use each word only once.

1. The _____ of short children on the team seemed unfair to Thomas.

2. The actress felt compelled to _____ herself from her fans.

3. They had to be careful when applying the _____ to the lawn.

4. The play had an unexpected _____.

5. Dinosaurs like the brontosaurus were considered _____.

© 2012 The Critical Thinking Co.™ • www.CriticalThinking.com • 800-458-4849

FOCUS: son, tort

PREFIX		ROOT		SUFFIX	
con-	with, together	**son**	sound	**-ance**	state, quality, act
dis-	apart, opposite of	**tort**	twist	**-ic**	like, related to
ultra-	beyond			**-ion**	an action or process; state, quality, act
uni-	one				

DIRECTIONS: In Column A, identify the parts of each word by circling roots and then underlining prefixes and suffixes. Match each word to its correct meaning from Column B.

COLUMN A	COLUMN B
1. <u>dis</u>(son)<u>ance</u> _____	a. a twisted shape or position
2. ultrasonic _____	b. as one voice
3. unison _____	c. lack of harmony; discord
4. contortion _____	d. to alter the shape or condition of
5. distort _____	e. related to a frequency of sound vibrations beyond the normal hearing range; high in frequency

DIRECTIONS: Choose the best word from Column A for each sentence. Use each word only once.

1. The acrobat's _____ was amazing to watch.

2. Animal trainers have used _____ whistles to train dogs and dolphins.

3. No one wanted to be his friend because he would _____ the truth to get his way.

4. The chorus sang the song in _____.

5. The _____ between the strings and horns made it difficult to listen to the performance.

© 2012 The Critical Thinking Co.™ • www.CriticalThinking.com • 800-458-4849

FOCUS: spec/spect, vis

PREFIX		ROOT		SUFFIX	
con-	with, together	**spec/**	look, examine	**i-fy**	to make, to act, to do
en-	in, into	**spect**		**-ible**	able to be
in-	in, into; not	**vis**	see	**-ion**	an action or process; state, quality, act
retro-	backward				

DIRECTIONS: In Column A, identify the parts of each word by circling roots and then underlining prefixes and suffixes. Match each word to its correct meaning from Column B.

COLUMN A

1. in(spec)t<u>ion</u> _____
2. retrospect _____
3. specify _____
4. envision _____
5. invisible _____

COLUMN B

a. to picture in the mind
b. impossible to see
c. to state in detail or name
d. the remembering of past events
e. the act of examining or reviewing

DIRECTIONS: Choose the best word from Column A for each sentence. Use each word only once.

1. The colorful brochures helped them _____ what Walt Disney World would be like.

2. Marina worked an hour cleaning her room and hoped that it would pass her mother's _____.

3. They asked him to _____ the exact time and place of his arrival at the train station.

4. It was so foggy that the house next door was _____.

5. In _____, the injured skier wished he had remained on the beginner's slope.

© 2012 The Critical Thinking Co.™ • www.CriticalThinking.com • 800-458-4849

FOCUS: miss/mitt, sect

PREFIX		ROOT		SUFFIX	
ad-	to, toward, near	**miss/**	send, let go	**-ance**	state, quality, act
dis-	apart, opposite of	**mitt**		**-ary**	that which; someone or something that belongs to; of, related to, one who
e-	out, away, from	**sect**	cut		
inter-	between, among			**-ion**	an action or process; state, quality, act
re-	back, again				

DIRECTIONS: In Column A, identify the parts of each word by circling roots and then underlining prefixes and suffixes. Match each word to its correct meaning from Column B.

COLUMN A

1. a d (m i t t) a n c e _____
2. e m i s s a r y _____
3. r e m i t t a n c e _____
4. d i s s e c t _____
5. i n t e r s e c t i o n _____

COLUMN B

a. the act of sending back money to pay
b. to cut apart piece by piece
c. entry
d. the place or point where two things cross each other
e. a representative of a country or group sent on a mission

DIRECTIONS: Choose the best word from Column A for each sentence. Use each word only once.

1. Bills can now be paid by electronic _____.

2. The children were told to cross the street only at the _____.

3. The botany class had already begun to _____ the flowers.

4. Each country sent an _____ to the world peace meeting.

5. The sign on the door clearly read, "No _____."

Extension Worksheet One

DIRECTIONS: Write the letter of the correct meaning for each word.

WORD		MEANING
1. infrastructure	_____	a. relating to the quality of being able to move
2. retract	_____	b. to formally break away from
3. convince	_____	c. a movement backward to an earlier state
4. commotion	_____	d. to go forward, especially after stopping
5. mobility	_____	e. to honor the memory of, as by a ceremony
6. secede	_____	f. underlying framework of a system
7. regression	_____	g. being, living, or used under water
8. commemorate	_____	h. to draw or pull back
9. submarine	_____	i. the scene of noisy confusion or activity
10. proceed	_____	j. to persuade by argument or evidence

This activity is a review of pages 1–7.

© 2012 The Critical Thinking Co.™ • www.CriticalThinking.com • 800-458-4849

Extension Worksheet Two

DIRECTIONS: Each line has only one word that is spelled correctly. Circle it.

1. acessible	accesible	accessible
2. pugnacious	pugnicious	pugacious
3. accelerate	acelerate	acselerate
4. recontruction	reconstrucsion	reconstruction
5. aqamarine	acuamarine	aquamarine
6. invencible	invinsible	invincible
7. abreviete	abbreviate	abbriviate
8. digression	digresion	diggression
9. removable	remoovable	remuveable
10. aviatrik	aviatrix	aveatrixs

This activity is a review of pages 1–7.

© 2012 The Critical Thinking Co.™ • www.CriticalThinking.com • 800-458-4849

Extension Worksheet Three

DIRECTIONS: Circle the word in parentheses that best fits the sentence.

1. There were thousands of people in attendance at the (removable, memorial) celebration for Dr. Martin Luther King, Jr.

2. The (aviary, aviatrix) contained many tropical birds.

3. The giant believed he was (invincible, pugnacious) until Jack chopped down the beanstalk.

4. The ice on the tracks caused the conductor to (decelerate, accelerate) the train when approaching curves.

5. The art assistant was surprised to hear of her (digression, promotion) to head artist.

6. The city ordered the (destruction, regression) of the old building since it had not been repaired in years.

7. The transit system became (immobile, invincible) due to extreme blizzard conditions.

8. Mrs. Miller taught children that chewing with their mouths open was (pugnacious, repugnant).

9. Because of the (brevity, contraction) of the first ball game, he was able to stay for the second one.

10. The (digression, obstruction) in her throat caused her to stop breathing.

This activity is a review of pages 1–7.

© 2012 The Critical Thinking Co.™ • www.CriticalThinking.com • 800-458-4849

Extension Worksheet Four

DIRECTIONS: Write the letter of the correct meaning for each word.

	WORD		**MEANING**
1.	inaudible	_____	a. an arrangement or putting together of parts
2.	counteract	_____	b. of or relating to the sense of touch
3.	circumvent	_____	c. process of acquiring knowledge
4.	intervene	_____	d. unable to be heard
5.	terminal	_____	e. a statement foretelling the future
6.	composition	_____	f. to act directly against; to prevent from affecting
7.	tactile	_____	g. to go around; to bypass restrictions
8.	circumscribe	_____	h. related to something leading to the end or to death
9.	prediction	_____	i. to come between; to intercede
10.	cognition	_____	j. to draw around; to encircle

This activity is a review of pages 8–14.

© 2012 The Critical Thinking Co.™ • www.CriticalThinking.com • 800-458-4849

Extension Worksheet Five

DIRECTIONS: Each line has only one word that is spelled correctly. Circle it.

1. exterminate   extermenite   extraerminate

2. curcumscribe   circimscrib   circumscribe

3. prescrepshun   prescription   priscripsion

4. recognize   recugnize   recogize

5. enaudible   inaudible   inadible

6. audience   audeince   adience

7. juvunile   juvenile   juvinile

8. corrupsion   corruption   coruption

9. counteract   conteract   countract

10. cunvention   convension   convention

This activity is a review of pages 8–14.

Extension Worksheet Six

DIRECTIONS: Choose a word from the box to fill in the blanks below. Use each word only once.

intercept	contradict	inscription	opposition	determination
interaction	rejuvenate	exterminate	imposition	intact

1. The boy's _____ to improve his grades was evident in his report card.

2. A good night's rest helped _____ the overworked accountant.

3. Scientists think that an asteroid helped _____ the dinosaurs.

4. The town's decision to open a new shopping mall met with a great deal of _____ .

5. The _____ on the old gravestone was nearly unreadable.

6. The teenager felt it was a great_____ to clean his room once a month.

7. Marianne was surprised that the vase was still _____ after it fell off the counter.

8. A student tried to _____ the note Sue was passing to Sean.

9. He did not want to _____ his friend Joan, but he felt he must tell the truth.

10. The teacher was pleased to observe the good _____ among the science teammates.

This activity is a review of pages 8–14.

 © 2012 The Critical Thinking Co.™ • www.CriticalThinking.com • 800-458-4849

Extension Worksheet Seven

DIRECTIONS: Write the letter of the correct meaning for each word.

WORD		MEANING
1. animate	_____	a. speaking beautifully and forcefully
2. equanimity	_____	b. to confirm; to prove to be true
3. eloquent	_____	c. calm temperament; evenness of temper
4. misnomer	_____	d. to give spirit, life, motion, or activity to
5. carnivorous	_____	e. having to do with the hands
6. contemporary	_____	f. to turn into or transform
7. fragment	_____	g. flesh-eating
8. manual	_____	h. a broken piece
9. convert	_____	i. of the same time; modern time
10. verify	_____	j. an error in naming a person or thing

This activity is a review of pages 15–22.

© 2012 The Critical Thinking Co.™ • www.CriticalThinking.com • 800-458-4849

Extension Worksheet Eight

DIRECTIONS: Each line has only one word that is spelled correctly. Circle it.

1. unilateral   unnlateral   uniladeral

2. nomenate   nominate   nomminate

3. fraggil   fragill   fragile

4. bicentennial   bisentenial   bicenteniel

5. intravertion   introvirsion   introversion

6. contemporary   contemptorary   contemperary

7. bennevolent   benevolent   benevulent

8. increadible   incredible   encredibile

9. infraction   infracsion   infracktion

10. loquacious   loqcuacious   locuatious

This activity is a review of pages 15–22.

© 2012 The Critical Thinking Co.™ • www.CriticalThinking.com • 800-458-4849

Extension Worksheet Nine

DIRECTIONS: Circle the word in parentheses that bests fits the sentence.

1. The little girl surprised everyone with her (extemporaneous, voracious) appetite.

2. Because of her outgoing and (unilateral, benevolent) personality, she was voted most likely to succeed.

3. Having lived for ten decades, the grandmother was honored with a (perennial, centennial) celebration.

4. A (deduction, production) of points would be taken if a music academy student did not practice daily.

5. Jeremy would be a good treasurer for the club because of his (veracity, equanimity).

6. Workers knew that the sandbags were only a (contemporary, temporary) solution to stopping the flood water.

7. He cleaned his room of his own (volition, abduction), instead of waiting to be told to do it.

8. The young man made a driving (infraction, fraction) the week after he received his driver's license.

9. The owner of the smashed car was (incredulous, unilateral) that no one witnessed the car accident on the busy street.

10. During a game, a soccer player will (verify, traverse) the field many times.

This activity is a review of pages 15–22.

© 2012 The Critical Thinking Co.™ • www.CriticalThinking.com • 800-458-4849

Extension Worksheet Ten

DIRECTIONS: Write the letter of the correct meaning for each word.

WORD		MEANING
1. cumulative	_____	a. the act of bringing back to life; renewed interest in
2. equivocate	_____	b. the act of examining or reviewing
3. revival	_____	c. the length of time something lasts
4. herbivorous	_____	d. lack of harmony; discord
5. inspection	_____	e. gradually building up
6. vociferous	_____	f. to use misleading language that could be interpreted in different ways
7. dissonance	_____	g. giving off or reflecting light
8. admittance	_____	h. plant-eating
9. duration	_____	i. entry
10. luminous	_____	j. loud; noisy

This activity is a review of pages 23–30.

© 2012 The Critical Thinking Co.™ • www.CriticalThinking.com • 800-458-4849

Extension Worksheet Eleven

DIRECTIONS: Each line has only one word that is spelled correctly. Circle it.

1. equasion   eqation   equation

2. iluminate   elluminate   illuminate

3. luminary   lumenary   lummenary

4. revockable   revoocable   revocable

5. exclussion   exclusion   excclusion

6. diccect   dissect   discect

7. remittance   remmittance   remittanse

8. emiccary   emessery   emissary

9. herbicide   erbicide   hurbicide

10. unisun   unision   unison

This activity is a review of pages 23–30.

© 2012 The Critical Thinking Co.™ • www.CriticalThinking.com • 800-458-4849

Extension Worksheet Twelve

DIRECTIONS: Choose a word from the box to fill in the blanks below. Use each word only once.

intersection	accumulate	contortion	inspection	innovation
seclude	equity	novice	ultrasonic	envision

1. Anne's goal was to _____ enough points in the game to win a prize.

2. The new legislature did a thorough _____ of the bylaws.

3. The acrobat made the _____ look easy to perform.

4. Until he has enough money to buy the red convertible, Phil can only _____ himself driving it.

5. The truck driver located the _____ of Highway 28 and Highway 60 on his map.

6. The best way to keep the two biggest guinea pigs calm is to _____ them from the others.

7. Even though Carmen was a _____, she won the card game.

8. The store scanner was an _____ that sped up the process of paying for groceries.

9. Maria saw the _____ in the plan that called for each child to take a turn cleaning the mouse cage.

10. Bats give off _____ calls to help them locate their food.

This activity is a review of pages 23–30.

© 2012 The Critical Thinking Co.™ • www.CriticalThinking.com • 800-458-4849

Independent Study

Building a Family of Words

Now that you have completed your studies in *Word Roots*, see how well you can do at forming words from any given root. Use as many reference sources as necessary.

DIRECTIONS: Below you will find five Latin roots, along with their meanings and a sample for each root. Add to each family of roots by forming as many additional words as you can.

1. **cap, cip, capt, cept**   take, hold

   capacity _____

   recipient _____

   captive _____

   deceptive _____

2. **spec, spic, spect**   look, examine

   speculate _____

   despicable _____

   spectrum _____

3. **scrib, script**   write, written

   scribble _____

   subscription _____

4. **sta, stat**   stand

   obstacle _____

   statutory _____

5. **vers, vert**   turn

   diversify _____

   convertible _____

Independent Study

Building a Family of Words

Now that you have completed your studies in *Word Roots*, see how well you can do at forming words from any given root. Use as many reference sources as necessary.

DIRECTIONS: Below you will find five Latin roots, along with their meanings and a sample word for each root. Add to each family of roots by forming as many additional words as you can.

1. **sens, sent**   feel

    sensational   _____

    resentment   _____

2. **pend, pens, pond**   hang, weigh, pay

    pendant   _____

    dispenser   _____

    imponderable   _____

3. **semble, simil, simul**   together, likeness, pretense

    resemblance   _____

    assimilate   _____

    simulator   _____

4. **ten, tent**   hold

    tenable   _____

    retention   _____

5. **miss, mitt**   send, let go

    dismissal   _____

    unremitting   _____

© 2012 The Critical Thinking Co.™ • www.CriticalThinking.com • 800-458-4849

Answer Key

Pretest/Posttest (p. vi)

Answers may vary.

1. **traverse**: to move across or turn back and forth across

2. **regression**: a movement backward to an earlier state

3. **brevity**: quality of being brief; shortness in time

4. **contradict**: to express or imply the opposite of

5. **pugnacious**: having a quarrelsome or aggressive nature

6. **postscript**: an addition to an already completed letter, article, or book

7. **cumulative**: gradually building up

8. **accelerate**: to increase the speed of

9. **animate**: to give spirit, life, motion, or activity to

10. **emissary**: a representative of a country or group sent on a mission

11. **loquacious**: very talkative

12. **envision**: to picture in the mind

13. **vociferous**: loud, noisy

14. **veracity**: truth, honesty

15. **infraction**: the act of breaking the limits or rules

Warm-Up Activity 1 (p. viii)

1. in nov ate
2. con tract ion
3. con vent ion
4. inter cept
5. nomin ate
6. re tract
7. ac celer ate
8. aqua mar ine
9. nomin al
10. nov ice

Warm-Up Activity 2 (p. ix)

1. inter, interact
2. counter, counteract
3. re, react
4. pro, progress
5. di, digress
6. ob, obstruct
7. con, construct
8. re, con, reconstruct

Warm-Up Activity 3 (p. x)

1. ous = luminous
2. ary = luminary
3. y = memory
4. able = memorable
5. al = memorial
6. il + ity = mobility
7. ion = motion
8. able = movable

Warm-Up Activity 4 (p. xi)

Definitions may vary.

1. to form by putting together parts
2. of or pertaining to the sea
3. easiy broken; delicate
4. too extraordinary and impossible to believe
5. to reduce the speed of
6. to stop or hinder by breaking in on
7. the end or last part
8. flesh-eating

Page 1

1. b   con struct
2. a   de struct ion
3. d   infra struct ure
4. e   ob struct ion
5. c   re con struct ion

1. destruction
2. obstruction
3. reconstruction
4. infrastructure
5. construct

Page 2

1. c   con tract ion
2. d   ex tract ion
3. e   re tract
4. b   con vince
5. a   in vinc ible

1. contraction
2. convince
3. extraction
4. invincible
5. retract

© 2012 The Critical Thinking Co.™ • www.CriticalThinking.com • 800-458-4849

Page 3

1. d　com(mot)ion
2. e　im(mob)ile
3. b　(mob)il ity
4. a　pro(mot)ion
5. c　re(mov)able
1. commotion
2. promotion
3. removable
4. mobility
5. immobile

Page 4

1. d　ab(brev)i ate
2. a　(brev)ity
3. c　ac(cess)ible
4. e　pro(ceed)
5. b　se(cede)
1. secede
2. proceed
3. brevity
4. abbreviate
5. accessible

Page 5

1. e　ac(celer)ate
2. a　de(celer)ate
3. b　di(gress)ion
4. c　pro(gress)
5. d　re(gress)ion
1. decelerate
2. digression
3. accelerate
4. progress
5. regression

Page 6

1. b　(avi)ary
2. c　(avia)trix
3. d　com(memor)ate
4. e　(memor)y
5. a　(memor)i al
1. aviary
2. commemorate
3. aviatrix
4. memory
5. memorial

Page 7

1. c　aqua(mar)ine
2. e　(mar)ine
3. d　sub(mar)ine
4. b　(pugn)acious
5. a　re(pugn)ant
1. marine
2. pugnacious
3. submarine
4. repugnant
5. aquamarine

Page 8

1. b　counter(act)
2. a　inter(act)ion
3. d　re(act)ion
4. c　(aud)i ence
5. e　in(aud)ible
1. reaction
2. interaction
3. audience
4. counteract
5. inaudible

Page 9

1. b　(juven)ile
2. d　re(juven)ate
3. c　circum(vent)
4. e　con(vent)ion
5. a　inter(vene)
1. circumvent
2. intervene
3. rejuvenate
4. juvenile
5. convention

Page 10

1. b　(cogn)i tion
2. a　re(cogn)ize
3. d　de(termin)ation
4. c　ex(termin)ate
5. e　(termin)al
1. terminal
2. determination
3. recognize
4. exterminate
5. cognition

Page 11

1. d　circum(scribe)
2. a　de(scribe)
3. c　in(script)ion
4. e　post(script)
5. b　pre(script)ion
1. postscript
2. circumscribe
3. inscription
4. prescription
5. describe

Page 12

1. c　inter(cept)
2. d　re(capt)ure
3. a　con(tact)
4. e　in(tact)
5. b　(tact)ile
1. intact
2. recapture
3. intercept

4. contact

5. tactile

Page 13

1. b contra⟨dict⟩

2. d pre⟨dict⟩ion

3. e cor⟨rupt⟩ion

4. a inter⟨rupt⟩

5. c ⟨rupt⟩ure

1. contradict

2. corruption

3. rupture

4. prediction

5. interrupt

Page 14

1. e ex⟨pose⟩

2. c com⟨posit⟩ion

3. b de⟨posit⟩

4. a im⟨posit⟩ion

5. d op⟨posit⟩ion

1. expose

2. opposition

3. deposit

4. composition

5. imposition

Page 15

1. d ⟨fract⟩ion

2. e ⟨fract⟩ure

3. b in⟨fract⟩ion

4. c ⟨frag⟩ile

5. a ⟨frag⟩ment

1. fraction

2. fragment

3. fragile

4. infraction

5. fracture

Page 16

1. a ⟨anim⟩ate

2. d ⟨equ⟩⟨anim⟩ity

3. e ⟨cred⟩ence

4. b in⟨cred⟩ible

5. c in⟨cred⟩ulous

1. incredible

2. incredulous

3. equanimity

4. credence

5. animate

Page 17

1. b ab⟨duct⟩ion

2. d de⟨duct⟩ion

3. a in⟨duct⟩

4. c bene⟨vol⟩ent

5. e ⟨vol⟩i tion

1. deduction

2. induct

3. abduction

4. benevolent

5. volition

Page 18

1. e a⟨vers⟩ion

2. d con⟨vert⟩

3. b extro⟨vert⟩

4. c intro⟨vers⟩ion

5. a tra⟨verse⟩

1. traverse

2. extrovert

3. aversion

4. convert

5. introversion

Page 19

1. e e⟨loqu⟩ent

2. a ⟨loqu⟩acious

3. c ⟨nomin⟩al

4. d ⟨nomin⟩ate

5. b mis⟨nom⟩er

1. nominate

2. misnomer

3. nominal

4. eloquent

5. loquacious

Page 20

1. c ⟨manu⟩al

2. e ⟨manu⟩script

3. a ⟨carn⟩i⟨vor⟩ous

4. d de⟨vour⟩

5. b ⟨vor⟩acious

1. voracious

2. manual

3. carnivorous

4. devour

5. manuscript

Page 21

1. b bi cent⟨enni⟩al

2. d cent⟨enni⟩al

3. e per⟨enni⟩al

4. c bi⟨later⟩al

5. a uni⟨later⟩al

1. perennial

2. bicentennial

3. bilateral

4. unilateral

5. centennial

Page 22

1. b con⟨tempor⟩ary

2. d ex⟨tempor⟩aneous

3. a ⟨tempor⟩ary

4. e ⟨ver⟩acity

5. c ⟨ver⟩i fy

1. extemporaneous
2. veracity
3. verify
4. temporary
5. contemporary

Page 23

1. e <u>dur</u>able
2. c <u>dur</u>ation
3. d re<u>viv</u>al
4. b <u>viv</u>acious
5. a <u>viv</u>id

1. vivid
2. vivacious
3. duration
4. revival
5. durable

Page 24

1. d ex<u>claim</u>
2. c pro<u>clam</u>ation
3. b <u>equ</u>ation
4. a <u>equ</u>ity
5. e <u>equi</u><u>voc</u>ate

1. equity
2. proclamation
3. exclaim
4. equation
5. equivocate

Page 25

1. c ac<u>cumul</u>ate
2. a <u>cumul</u>at <u>ive</u>
3. b il<u>lumin</u>ate
4. e <u>lumin</u>ary
5. d <u>lumin</u>ous

1. luminous
2. cumulative
3. accumulate

4. luminary
5. illuminate

Page 26

1. c in<u>nov</u>ation
2. d <u>nov</u>ice
3. a re<u>nov</u>ate
4. e re<u>voc</u>able
5. b <u>voci</u>ferous

1. revocable
2. renovate
3. innovation
4. vociferous
5. novice

Page 27

1. b con<u>clus</u>ion
2. d ex<u>clus</u>ion
3. c se<u>clude</u>
4. e <u>herbi</u><u>cide</u>
5. a <u>herbi</u><u>vor</u>ous

1. exclusion
2. seclude
3. herbicide
4. conclusion
5. herbivorous

Page 28

1. c dis<u>son</u>ance
2. e ultra<u>son</u>ic
3. b uni<u>son</u>
4. a con<u>tort</u>ion
5. d dis<u>tort</u>

1. contortion
2. ultrasonic
3. distort
4. unison
5. dissonance

Page 29

1. e in<u>spect</u>ion
2. d retro<u>spect</u>
3. c <u>spec</u>i <u>fy</u>
4. a en<u>vis</u>ion
5. b in<u>vis</u>ible

1. envision
2. inspection
3. specify
4. invisible
5. retrospect

Page 30

1. c ad<u>mitt</u>ance
2. e e<u>miss</u>ary
3. a re<u>mitt</u>ance
4. b dis<u>sect</u>
5. d inter<u>sect</u>ion

1. remittance
2. intersection
3. dissect
4. emissary
5. admittance

Extension Worksheets
Worksheet One (p. 31)

1. f   6. b
2. h   7. c
3. j   8. e
4. i   9. g
5. a   10. d

Worksheet Two (p. 32)

1. accessible (3rd)
2. pugnacious (1st)
3. accelerate (1st)
4. reconstruction (3rd)
5. aquamarine (3rd)
6. invincible (3rd)

7. abbreviate (2nd)
8. digression (1st)
9. removable (1st)
10. aviatrix (2nd)

Worksheet Three (p. 33)

1. memorial
2. aviary
3. invincible
4. decelerate
5. promotion
6. destruction
7. immobile
8. repugnant
9. brevity
10. obstruction

Worksheet Four (p. 34)

1. d   6. a
2. f   7. b
3. g   8. j
4. i   9. e
5. h   10. c

Worksheet Five (p. 35)

1. exterminate (1st)
2. circumscribe (3rd)
3. prescription (2nd)
4. recognize (1st)
5. inaudible (2nd)
6. audience (1st)
7. juvenile (2nd)
8. corruption (2nd)
9. counteract (1st)
10. convention (3rd)

Worksheet Six (p. 36)

1. determination
2. rejuvenate
3. exterminate
4. opposition
5. inscription
6. imposition
7. intact
8. intercept
9. contradict
10. interaction

Worksheet Seven (p. 37)

1. d   6. i
2. c   7. h
3. a   8. e
4. j   9. f
5. g   10. b

Worksheet Eight (p. 38)

1. unilateral (1st)
2. nominate (2nd)
3. fragile (3rd)
4. bicentennial (1st)
5. introversion (3rd)
6. contemporary (1st)
7. benevolent (2nd)
8. incredible (2nd)
9. infraction (1st)
10. loquacious (1st)

Worksheet Nine (p. 39)

1. voracious
2. benevolent
3. centennial
4. deduction
5. veracity
6. temporary

7. volition
8. infraction
9. incredulous
10. traverse

Worksheet Ten (p. 40)

1. e   6. j
2. f   7. d
3. a   8. i
4. h   9. c
5. b   10. g

Worksheet Eleven (p. 41)

1. equation (3rd)
2. illuminate (3rd)
3. luminary (1st)
4. revocable (3rd)
5. exclusion (2nd)
6. dissect (2nd)
7. remittance (1st)
8. emissary (3rd)
9. herbicide (1st)
10. unison (3rd)

Worksheet Twelve (p. 42)

1. accumulate
2. inspection
3. contortion
4. envision
5. intersection
6. seclude
7. novice
8. innovation
9. equity
10. ultrasonic

Independent Study (pp. 43–44)

Answers will vary.

DICTIONARY OF LATIN PREFIXES

a- away, from; not, without
aversion: the act of turning away from; a dislike of something [ə-vûr-zhən]

ab- away, from
abbreviate: to shorten [ə-brē′vē-āt′]
abduction: a taking away by force [ăb-dŭk′-tion]

ac- to, toward, near
accelerate: to increase the speed of [ăk-sĕl′-ə-rāt′]
accessible: easily entered, approached, or obtained [ăk-sĕs′-ə-bəl]
accumulate: to gather or pile up little by little [ə-kyoom′-yə-lāt′]

ad- to, toward, near
admittance: entry [ăd-mĭt′-ns]

bene- good, well
benevolent: showing kindness or goodwill [bə-nĕv′-ə-lənt]

bi- two
bicentennial: of or relating to an age or period of 200 years [bī′-sĕn-tĕn′-ē-əl]
bilateral: of or involving two sides; reciprocal [bī-lăt′-ər-əl]

cent- hundred
centennial: of or relating to an age or period of 100 years [sĕn-tĕn′-ē-əl]

circum- around
circumscribe: to draw around; to encircle [sûr′-kəm-skrīb′]
circumvent: to go around; to bypass restrictions [sûr′-kəm-vĕnt′]

com- with, together
commemorate: to honor the memory of, as by a ceremony [kə-mĕm′-ə-rāt′]
commotion: the scene of noisy confusion or activity [kə-mō′-shən]
composition: an arrangement or putting together of parts [kŏm′-pə-zĭsh′-ən]

con- with, together
conclusion: the end or last part [kən-kloo′-zhən]

construct: to form by putting together parts [kən-strŭkt′]
contact: the state of touching or meeting [kŏn′-tăkt′]
contemporary: of the same time; modern time [kən-tĕm′-pə-rĕr′-ē]
contortion: a twisted shape or position [kən-tôr′-shən]
contraction: act of drawing together or shrinking [kən-trăk′-shən]
convention: a gathering or assembly of people with a common interest [kən-vĕn′-shən]
convert: to turn into or transform [kən-vûrt′]
convince: to persuade by argument or evidence [kən-vĭns′]

contra- against, opposite
contradict: to express or imply the opposite of [kŏn′-trə-dĭkt′]

cor- with, together
corruption: a break with what is loegally or morally right [kuh-rup′-shun]

counter- against, opposite
counteract: to act directly against; to prevent from affecting [koun′-tər-ăkt′]

de- from, away, down; apart; not
decelerate: to reduce the speed of [dē-sĕl′-ə-rāt′]
deduction: a subtraction of an amount [dĭ-dŭk′-shən]
deposit: to put down or in a safe place [dĭ-pŏz′-ĭt]
describe: to represent with words or pictures [dĭ-skrīb′]
destruction: the act of destroying; a state of damage [dĭ-strŭk′-shən]
determination: an intent to reach a goal [dĭ-tûr′-mə-nā′-shən]
devour: to eat quickly [dĭ-vour′]

di- apart, away; not
digression: a departure from the main issue, subject, etc. [dī-grĕsh′ən]

dis- apart, opposite of
dissect: to cut apart piece by piece [dĭ-sĕkt′]
disruptive: tending towards a break in the normal course or process [dĭs-rŭp′tĭv]
dissonance: lack of harmony; discord [dĭs′-ə-nəns]
distort: to alter the shape or condition of [dĭ-stôrt′]

e- out, away, from
eloquent: speaking beautifully and forcefully [ĕl′-ə-kwənt]
emissary: a representative of a country or group sent on a mission [ĕm′-ĭ-sĕr′-ē]

en- in, into
envision: to picture in the mind [ĕn-vĭzh′-ən]

ex- out, away, from
exclaim: to cry out or speak in a strong or sudden manner [ĭk-sklām′]
exclusion: a shutting out; rejection [ĭk-skloo′-zhən]
expose: to place something where it can be seen; to put in an unprotected situation [ĭk-spōz′]
extemporaneous: done without any preparation; impromptu [ĭk-stĕm′-pə-rā′-nē-əs]
exterminate: to destroy or get rid of completely [ĭk-stûr′-mə-nāt′]
extraction: process of withdrawing, pulling out [ĭk-străk′-shən]

extro- outside of
extrovert: an outgoing person [ĕk′-strə-vûrt′]

il- in, into; not
illuminate: to give light to [ĭ-loo′-mə-nāt′]

im- in, into; not
immobile: motionless; unable to move [ĭ-mō′-bəl]
imposition: an excessive or unjust burden placed on someone [ĭm′-pə-zĭsh′-ən]

in- in, into; not
inaudible: unable to be heard [ĭn-o′-də-bəl]
incredible: too extraordinary and impossible to believe [ĭn-krĕd′-ə-bəl]
incredulous: disbelieving; not believing [ĭn-krĕj′-ə-ləs]
induct: to formally install someone to an office or position [ĭn-dŭkt′]
infraction: the act of breaking the limits or rules [ĭn-frăk′-shən]
innovation: a new idea, method, or device [ĭn′-ə-vā′-shən]
inscription: an engraving on a coin or other object [ĭn-skrĭp′-shən]
inspection: the act of examining or reviewing [ĭn-spĕk′-shən]
intact: with nothing missing; left whole [ĭn-tăkt′]
invincible: unbeatable; impossible to overcome [ĭn-vĭn′-sə-bəl]
invisible: impossible to see [ĭn-vĭz′-ə-bəl]

infra- beneath
infrastructure: underlying framework of a system [ĭn′-frə-strŭk′-chər]

inter- between, among
interaction: communication between two or more things [ĭn′-tər-ăk′-shən]
intercept: to stop or interrupt the course of [ĭn′-tər-sĕpt′]
interrupt: to stop or hinder by breaking in on [ĭn′-tə-rŭpt′]
intersection: the place or point where two things cross each other [ĭn′-tər-sĕk′-shən]
intervene: to come between; to intercede [ĭn′-tər-vēn′]

intro- within
introversion: turning inward; focusing on oneself [ĭn′-trə-vur′-zhən]

mis- bad, wrong
misnomer: an error in naming a person or thing [mĭs-nō′-mər]

ob- to, toward, against
obstruction: an obstacle or something put up against something else [əb-strŭk′-shən]

© 2012 The Critical Thinking Co.™ • www.CriticalThinking.com • 800-458-4849

op-   to, toward, against
opposition: the act of resistance or action against [ŏp'-ə-zĭsh'-ən]

per-   through, very
perennial: lasting through many years [pə-rĕn'-ē-əl]

post-   after
postscript: an addition to an already completed letter, article, or book [pōst'-skrĭpt']

pre-   before, in front of
prediction: a statement foretelling the future [prĭ-dĭk'-shən]
prescription: a written order for medicine [prĭ-skrĭp'-shən]

pro-   for, before, forward
proceed: to go forward, especially after stopping [prō-sēd']
proclamation: something announced officially in public [prŏk'-lə-mā'-shən]
progress: movement forward or onward; improvement [prŏg'-rĕs']
promotion: an advancement in rank or position [prə-mō'-shən]

re-   back, again
reaction: a response [rē-ăk'-shən]
recapture: the taking back of something [rē-kăp'-chər]
recognize: to identify someone or something seen before [rĕk'-əg-nīz']
reconstruction: the act of putting back together [rē'-kən-strŭk'-shən]
regression: a movement backward to an earlier state [rĭ-grĕsh'-ən]
rejuvenate: to bring back to youthful strength or appearance [rĭ-jōō'-və-nāt']
remittance: the act of sending back money to pay [rĭ-mĭt'-ns]
removable: able to be taken or carried away [rĭ-mōō'-və-bəl]
renovate: to make something like new again [rĕn'-ə-vāt']
repugnant: distasteful; offensive or revolting [rĭ-pŭg'-nənt]
retract: to draw or pull back [rĭ-trăkt']
revival: the act of bringing back to life; renewed interest in [rĭ-vī'-vəl]

revocable: able to be repealed or withdrawn [rĕv'-ə-kə-bəl]

retro-   backward
retrospect: the remembering of past events [rĕt'-rə-spĕkt']

se-   apart, aside
secede: to formally break away from [sĭ-sēd']
seclude: to keep away from; to isolate [sĭ-klōōd']

sub-   under, below
submarine: being, living, or used under water [sŭb'-mə-rēn']

tra-   across, through
traverse: to move across or turn back and forth across [trə-vurs']

ultra-   beyond
ultrasonic: related to a frequency of sound vibrations beyond the normal hearing range; high in frequency [ŭl'-trə-sŏn'-ĭk]

uni-   one
unilateral: affecting one side of something [yōō'-nə-lăt'-ər-əl]
unison: as one voice [yōō'-nĭ-sən]

    © 2012 The Critical Thinking Co.™ • www.CriticalThinking.com • 800-458-4849

DICTIONARY OF LATIN ROOTS

act   to do, to drive
counteract: to act directly against; to prevent from affecting [koun'-tər-ăkt']
interaction: communication between two or more things [ĭn'-tər-ăk'-shən]
reaction: a response [rē-ăk'-shən]

anim   spirit, life
animate: to give spirit, life, motion, or activity to [ăn'-ə-māt']
equanimity: calm temperament; evenness of temper [ĕ'-kwə-nĭm'-ĭ-tē]

aqua   water
aquamarine: blue-green in color, like sea water [ăk'-wə-mə-rēn']

aud   hear
audience: a group of listeners or spectators [ô'-dē-əns]
inaudible: unable to be heard [ĭn-ô'-də-bəl]

avi   bird
aviary: a large enclosure in which birds are kept [ā'-vē-ĕr'-ē]

avia   bird
aviatrix: a woman airplane pilot [ā'-vē-ā'-trĭks]

brev   short
abbreviate: to shorten [ə-brē'-vē-āt']
brevity: quality of being brief; shortness in time [brĕv'-ĭ-tē]

capt   take, hold
recapture: the taking back of something [rē-kăp'-chər]

carni   flesh, meat
carnivorous: flesh-eating [kär-nĭv'-ər-əs]

cede   go, yield
secede: to formally break away from [sĭ-sēd']

ceed   go, yield
proceed: to go forward, especially after stopping [prō-sēd']

celer   fast
accelerate: to increase the speed of [ăk-sĕl'-ə-rāt']
decelerate: to reduce the speed of [dē-sĕl'-ə-rāt']

cept   take, hold
intercept: to stop or interrupt the course of [ĭn'-tər-sĕpt']

cess   go, yield
accessible: easily entered, approached, or obtained [ăk-sĕs'-ə-bəl]

claim   call out, shout
exclaim: to cry out or speak in a strong or sudden manner [ĭk-sklām']

clam   call out, shout
proclamation: something announced officially in public [prŏk'-lə-mā'-shən]

clude   close
seclude: to keep away from; to isolate [sĭ-klood']

clus   close
conclusion: the end or last part [kən-kloo'-zhən]
exclusion: a shutting out; rejection [ĭk-skloo'-zhən]

cogn   know
cognition: process of acquiring knowledge [kŏg-nĭsh'-ən]
recognize: to identify someone or something seen before [rĕk'-əg-nīz']

cred   believe
credence: belief; acceptance as true or valid [krĕd'-ns]
incredible: too extraordinary and impossible to believe [ĭn-krĕd'-ə-bəl]
incredulous: disbelieving; not believing [ĭn-krĕj'-ə-ləs]

cumul   mass, heap
accumulate: to gather or pile up little by little [ə-kyoom'-yə-lāt']
cumulative: gradually building up [kyoom'-yə-lə'-tĭv]

© 2012 The Critical Thinking Co.™ • www.CriticalThinking.com • 800-458-4849

dict say, speak
contradict: to express or imply the opposite of [kŏn'-trə-dĭkt']
prediction: a statement foretelling the future [prĭ-dĭk'-shən]

duct lead
abduction: a taking away by force [ăb-dŭk'-shən]
deduction: a subtraction of an amount [dĭ-dŭk'-shən]
induct: to formally install someone to an office or position [ĭn-dŭkt']

dur harden, to last, lasting
durable: having the quality of lasting [door'-ə-bəl]
duration: the length of time something lasts [doo-rā'-shən]

enni year
bicentennial: of or relating to an age or period of 200 years [bī'-sĕn-tĕn'-ē-əl]
centennial: of or relating to an age or period of 100 years [sĕn-tĕn'-ē-əl]
perennial: lasting through many years [pə-rĕn'-ē-əl]

equ equal, fair
equanimity: calm temperament, evenness of temper [ĕ'-kwə-nĭm-'ĭ-tē]
equation: a statement of equality [ĭ-kwā'-zhən]
equity: fairness; the state of being just or fair [ĕk'-wĭ-tē]

equi (combining form) equal, fair
equivocate: to use misleading language that could be interpreted two different ways [ĭ-kwĭv'-ə-kāt']

fract break
fraction: a part or element of a larger whole [frăk'-shən]
fracture: a break, crack, or split [frăk'-chər]
infraction: the act of breaking the limits or rules [ĭn-frăk'-shən]

frag break
fragile: easily broken; delicate [frăj'-əl]

fragment: a broken piece [frăg'-mənt]

gress step
digression: a departure from the main issue, subject, etc. [dī-grĕsh'-ən]
progress: movement forward or onward; improvement [prŏg'-rĕs']
regression: a movement backward to an earlier state [rĭ-grĕsh'-ən]

herbi grass
herbicide: any chemical used to kill unwanted plants, etc. [hûr'-bĭ-sīd']
herbivorous: plant-eating [hur-bĭv'-ər-əs]

juven young
juvenile: youthful or childish; immature [joo'-və-nīl']
rejuvenate: to bring back to youthful strength or appearance [rĭ-joo'-və-nāt']

later side
bilateral: of or involving two sides; reciprocal [bī-lăt'-ər-əl]
unilateral: affecting one side of something [yoo'-nə-lăt'-ər-əl]

loqu speak
eloquent: speaking beautifully and forcefully [ĕl'-ə-kwənt]
loquacious: very talkative [lō-kwā'-shəs]

lumin light
illuminate: to give light to [ĭ-loo'-mə-nāt']
luminary: an object, like a star, that gives off light; a famous person (a "star") [loo'-mə-nĕr'-ē]
luminous: giving off or reflecting light [loo'-mə-nəs]

manu hand
manual: having to do with the hands [măn'-yoo-əl]
manuscript: a handwritten document or author's original text [măn'-yə-skrĭpt']

mar sea
aquamarine: blue-green in color, like

© 2012 The Critical Thinking Co.™ • www.CriticalThinking.com • 800-458-4849

sea water [ăk'-wə-mə-rēn']
marine: of or pertaining to the sea [mə-rēn']
submarine: being, living, or used under water [sŭb'-mə-rēn']

memor   remember
commemorate: to honor the memory of, as by a ceremony [kə-měm'-ə-rāt']
memorial: related to remembering a person or event [mə-môr'-ē-əl]
memory: an ability to retain knowledge; an individual's stock of retained knowledge [měm'-ə-rē]

miss   send, let go
emissary: a representative of a country or group sent on a mission [ĕm'-ĭ-sĕr'-ē]

mitt   send, let go
admittance: entry [ăd-mĭt'-ns]
remittance: the act of sending back money to pay [rĭ-mĭt'-ns]

mob   move
immobile: motionless; unable to move [ĭ-mō'-bəl]
mobility: relating to the quality of being able to move [mō-bĭl'-i-tē]

mot   move
commotion: the scene of noisy confusion or activity [kə-mō'-shən]
promotion: an advancement in rank or position [prə-mō'-shən]

mov   move
removable: able to be taken or carried away [rĭ-moo'-və-bəl]

nom   name
misnomer: an error in naming a person or thing [mĭs-nō'-mər]

nomin   name
nominal: being something in name only but not in reality [nŏm'-ə-nəl]
nominate: to name for election or appointment; to designate [nŏm'-ə-nāt']

nov   new
innovation: a new idea, method, or

device [ĭn'-ə-vā'-shən]
novice: a person who is new to an activity; a beginner [nŏv'-ĭs]
renovate: to make something like new again [rĕn'-ə-vāt']

pose   place, put
expose: to place something where it can be seen; to put in an unprotected situation [ĭk-spōz']

posit   place, put
composition: an arrangement or putting together of parts [kŏm'-pə-zĭsh'-ən]
deposit: to put down or in a safe place [dĭ-pŏz'-ĭt]
imposition: an excessive or unjust burden placed on someone [ĭm'-pə-zĭsh'-ən]
opposition: the act of resistance or action against [ŏp'-ə-zĭsh'-ən]

pugn   fight
pugnacious: having a quarrelsome or aggressive nature [pŭg-nā'-shəs]
repugnant: distasteful; offensive or revolting [rĭ-pŭg'-nənt]

rupt   break, burst
corruption: a break with what is legally or morally right [kuh- rup'-shun]
disruptive: tending towards a break in the normal course or process [dĭs-rŭp'-tĭv]
interrupt: to stop or hinder by breaking in on [ĭn'-tə-rŭpt']
rupture: a breaking apart or the state of being broken apart [rŭp'-chər]

scribe   write, written
circumscribe: to draw around; to encircle [sur'-kəm-skrīb']
describe: to represent with words or pictures [dĭ-skrīb']

script   write, written
inscription: an engraving on a coin or other object [ĭn-skrĭp'-shən]
manuscript: a handwritten document or author's original text [măn'-yə-skrĭpt']

postscript: an addition to an already completed letter, article, or book [pōst'-skrĭpt']

prescription: a written order for medicine [prĭ-skrĭp'-shən]

sect cut

dissect: to cut apart piece by piece [dĭ-sĕkt']

intersection: the place or point where two things cross each other [ĭn'-tər-sĕk'-shən]

son sound

dissonance: lack of harmony; discord [dĭs'-ə-nəns]

ultrasonic: related to a frequency of sound vibrations beyond the normal hearing range; high frequency [ŭl'-trə-sŏn'-ĭk]

unison: as one voice [yōō'-nĭ-sən]

spec look, examine

specify: to describe in detail [spĕs'-ə-fī']

spect look, examine

inspection: the act of examining or reviewing [ĭn-spĕk'-shən]

retrospect: the remembering of past events [rĕt'-rə-spĕkt']

struct build

construct: to form by putting together parts [kən-strŭkt']

destruction: the act of destroying; a state of damage [dĭ-strŭk'-shən]

infrastructure: underlying framework of a system [ĭn'-frə-strŭk'-chər]

obstruction: an obstacle or something put up against something else [əb-strŭk'-shən]

reconstruction: the act of putting back together [rē'-kən-strŭk'-shən]

tact touch

contact: the state of touching or meeting [kŏn'-tăkt']

intact: with nothing missing; left whole [ĭn-tăkt']

tactile: of or relating to the sense of touch [tăk'-təl]

tempor time

contemporary: of the same time; modern time [kən-tĕm'-pə-rĕr'-ē]

extemporaneous: done without preparation; impromptu [ĭk-stĕm'-pə-rā'-nē-əs]

temporary: lasting for a limited time [tĕm'-pə-rĕr'-ē]

termin end, limit

determination: an intent to reach a goal [dĭ-tûr'-mə-nā'-shən]

exterminate: to destroy or get rid of completely [ĭk-stûr'-mə-nāt']

terminal: related to something leading to the end or to death [tûr'-mə-nəl]

tort twist

contortion: a twisted shape or position [kən-tôr'-shən]

distort: to alter the shape or condition of [dĭ-stôrt']

tract to draw or pull, drag, draw out

contraction: act of drawing together or shrinking [kən-trăk'-shən]

extraction: process of withdrawing, pulling out [ĭk-străk'-shən]

retract: to draw or pull back [rĭ-trăkt']

vene come

intervene: to come between; to intercede [ĭn'-tər-vēn']

vent come

circumvent: to go around; to bypass restrictions [sûr'-kəm-vĕnt']

convention: a gathering or assembly of people with a common interest [kən-vĕn'-shən]

ver truth

veracity: truth, honesty [və-răs'-ĭ-tē]

verify: to confirm; to prove to be true [vĕr'-ə-fī]

vers turn

aversion: the act of turning away from; a dislike of something [ə-vûr'-zhən]

introversion: turning inward; focusing on oneself [ĭn'-trə-vûr'-zhən]

© 2012 The Critical Thinking Co.™ • www.CriticalThinking.com • 800-458-4849

verse	**traverse**: to move across or turn back and forth across [trə-vûrs']
vert	turn **convert**: to turn into or transform [kən-vûrt'] **extrovert**: an outgoing person [ĕk'-strə-vûrt']
vinc	conquer **invincible**: unbeatable; impossible to overcome [ĭn-vĭn'-sə-bəl]
vince	conquer **convince**: to persuade by argument or evidence [kən-vĭns']
vis	see **envision**: to picture in the mind [ĕn-vĭzh'-ən] **invisible**: impossible to see [ĭn-vĭz'-ə-bəl]
viv	live, life **revival**: the act of bringing back to life; renewed interest in [rĭ-vī'-vəl] **vivacious**: high-spirited and full of life [vĭ-vā'-shəs] **vivid**: lively in appearance; vigorous [vĭv'-ĭd]

voc	voice, call **equivocate**: to use misleading language that could be interpreted two different ways [ĭ-kwĭv'-ə-kāt'] **revocable**: able to be repealed or withdrawn [rĕv'-ə-kə-bəl]
voci	voice, call **vociferous**: loud, noisy [vō-sĭf'-ər-əs]
vol	will, wish **benevolent**: showing kindness or goodwill [bə-nĕv'-ə-lənt] **volition**: the act of making a choice or decision [və-lĭsh'-ən]
vor	eat **carnivorous**: flesh-eating [kär-nĭv'-ər-əs] **herbivorous**: plant-eating [hur-bĭv'-ər-əs] **voracious**: desiring or eating food in great quantities [vô-rā'-shəs]
vour	eat **devour**: to eat quickly [dĭ-vour']

DICTIONARY OF LATIN SUFFIXES

-able	able to be **durable**: having the quality of lasting [door'-ə-bəl] **removable**: able to be taken or carried away [rĭ-moo'-və-bəl] **revocable**: able to be repealed or withdrawn [rĕv'-ə-kə-bəl]
-acious	having the quality of **loquacious**: very talkative [lō-kwā'-shəs] **pugnacious**: having a quarrelsome or aggressive nature [pŭg-nā'-shəs] **vivacious**: high-spirited and full of life [vĭ-vā'-shəs] **voracious**: desiring or eating food in great quantities [vô-rā'-shəs]
-acity	the quality of **veracity**: truth, honesty [və-răs'-ĭ-tē]
-al	of, related to; an action or process **bilateral**: of or involving two sides; reciprocal [bī-lăt'-ər-əl]

	manual: having to do with the hands [măn'-yoo-əl] **nominal**: being something in name only but not in reality [nŏm'-ə-nəl] **revival**: the act of bringing back to life; renewed interest in [rĭ-vī'-vəl] **terminal**: related to something leading to the end or to death [tur'-mə-nəl] **unilateral**: affecting one side of something [yoo'-nə-lăt'-ər-əl]
i-al	of, related to; an action or process **bicentennial**: of or relating to an age or period of 200 years [bī'-sĕn-tĕn'-ē-əl] **centennial**: of or relating to an age or period of 100 years [sĕn-tĕn'-ē-əl] **memorial**: related to remembering a person or event [mə-môr'-ē-əl] **perennial**: lasting through many years [pə-rĕn'-ē-əl]

-ance   state, quality, act
admittance: entry [ăd-mĭt′-ns]
dissonance: lack of harmony; discord [dĭs′-ə-nəns]
remittance: the act of sending money back to pay [rĭ-mĭt′-ns]

-aneous   having the quality of
extemporaneous: done without preparation; impromptu [ĭk-stĕm′-pə-rā′-nē-əs]

-ant   one who, that which ; state, quality
repugnant: distasteful; offensive or revolting [rĭ-pŭg′-nənt]

-ary   that which; of, related to ; one who; someone or something that belongs to
aviary: a large enclosure in which birds are kept [ā′-vē-ĕr′-ē]
contemporary: of the same time; modern time [kən-tĕm′-pə-rĕr′-ē]
emissary: a representative of a country or group sent on a mission [ĕm′-ĭ-sĕr′-ē]
luminary: an object, like a star, that gives off light; a famous person (a "star") [lōō′-mə-nĕr-′ē]
temporary: lasting for a limited time [tĕm′-pə-rĕr′-ē]

-ate   to make, to act; one who, that which
accelerate: to increase the speed of [ăk-sĕl′-ə-rāt′]
accumulate: to gather or pile up little by little [ə-kyōōm′-yə-lāt′]
animate: to give spirit, life, motion, or activity to [ăn′-ə-māt′]
commemorate: to honor the memory of, as by a ceremony [kə-mĕm′-ə-rāt′]
decelerate: to reduce the speed of [dē-sĕl′-ə-rāt′]
equivocate: to use misleading language that could be interpreted two different ways [ĭ-kwĭv′-ə-kāt′]
exterminate: to destroy or get rid of completely [ĭk-stûr′-mə-nāt′]
illuminate: to give light to [ĭ-lōō′-mə-nāt′]
nominate: to name for election or appointment; to designate [nŏm′-ə-nāt′]

rejuvenate: to bring back to youthful strength or appearance [rĭ-jōō′-və-nāt′]
renovate: to make something like new again [rĕn′-ə-vāt′]

i-ate   to make, to act; one who, that which
abbreviate: to shorten [ə-brē′-vē-āt′]

-ation   an action or process
determination: an intention to reach a goal [dĭ-tûr′-mə-nā′-shən]
duration: the length of time something lasts [dōō-rā′-shən]
equation: a statement of equality [ĭ-kwā′-zhən]
innovation: a new idea, method, or device [ĭn′-ə-vā′-shən]
proclamation: something announced officially in public [prŏk′-lə-mā′-shən]

-cide   kill
herbicide: any chemical used to kill unwanted plants, etc. [hûr′-bĭ-sīd′]

-ence   state, quality, act
credence: belief; acceptance as true or valid [krĕd′-ns]

i-ence   state, quality, act
audience: a group of listeners or spectators [o′-dē-əns]

-ent   one who, that which, like, related to
benevolent: showing kindness or goodwill [bə-nĕv′-ə-lənt]
eloquent: speaking beautifully and forcefully [ĕl′-ə-kwənt]

-er   one who, that which
misnomer: an error in naming a person or thing [mĭs-nō′-mər]

-ferous   producing
vociferous: loud, noisy [vō-sĭf′-ər-əs]

i-fy   to make, to act, to do
specify: describe in detail [spĕs′-ə-fī′]
verify: to confirm; to prove to be true [vĕr′-ə-fī]

-ible   able to be
accessible: easily entered, approached, or obtained [ăk-sĕs′-ə-bəl]

© 2012 The Critical Thinking Co.™ • www.CriticalThinking.com • 800-458-4849

inaudible: unable to be heard [ĭn-o'-də-bəl]

incredible: too extraordinary and impossible to believe [ĭn-krĕd'-ə-bəl]

invincible: unbeatable; impossible to overcome [ĭn-vĭn'-sə-bəl]

invisible: impossible to see [ĭn-vĭz'-ə-bəl]

-ic   like, related to

ultrasonic: related to a frequency of sound vibrations beyond the normal hearing range; high frequency [ŭl'-trə-sŏn'ĭk]

-ice   one who, that which

novice: a person who is new to an activity; a beginner [nŏv'-ĭs]

-id   like, related to

vivid: lively in appearance; vigorous [vĭv'-ĭd]

-ile   like, of, relating to

fragile: easily broken; delicate [frăj'-əl]

immobile: motionless; unable to move [ĭ-mō'-bəl]

juvenile: youthful or childish; immature [jōō'-və-nīl']

tactile: of or relating to the sense of touch [tăk'-təl]

-ine   like, related to

aquamarine: blue-green in color, like sea water [ăk'-wə-mə-rēn']

marine: of or pertaining to the sea [mə-rēn']

submarine: being, living, or used under water [sŭb'-mə-rēn']

-ion   an action or process; state, quality, act

abduction: a taking away by force [ăb-dŭk'-tion]

aversion: the act of turning away from; a dislike of something [ə-vûr'-zhən]

commotion: the scene of noisy confusion or activity [kə-mō'-shən]

composition: an arrangement or putting together of parts [kŏm'-pə-zĭsh'-ən]

conclusion: the end or last part [kən-klōō'-zhən]

contortion: a twisted shape or position [kən-tor'-shən]

contraction: act of drawing together or shrinking [kən-trăk'-shən]

convention: a gathering or assembly of people with a common interest [kən-vĕn'-shən]

corruption: a break with what is legally or morally right [kuh-rup'-shun]

deduction: a subtraction of an amount [dĭ-dŭk'-shən]

destruction: the act of destroying; a state of damage [dĭ-strŭk'-shən]

digression: a departure from the main issue, subject, etc. [dī-grĕsh'-ən]

envision: to picture in the mind [ĕn-vĭzh'-ən]

exclusion: a shutting out; rejection [ĭk-sklōō'-zhən]

extraction: process of withdrawing, pulling out [ĭk-străk'-shən]

fraction: a part or element of a larger whole [frăk'-shən]

imposition: an excessive or unjust burden placed on someone [ĭm'-pə-zĭsh'-ən]

infraction: the act of breaking the limits or rules [ĭn-frăk'-shən]

inscription: an engraving on a coin or other object [ĭn-skrĭp'-shən]

inspection: the act of examining or reviewing [ĭn-spĕk'-shən]

interaction: communication between two or more things [ĭn'-tər-ăk'-shən]

intersection: the place or point where two things cross each other [ĭn'-tər-sĕk'-shən]

introversion: turning inward; focusing on oneself [ĭn'-trə-vûr'-zhən]

obstruction: an obstacle or something put up against something else [əb-strŭk'-shən]

opposition: the act of resistance or action against [ŏp'-ə-zĭsh'-ən]

prediction: a statement foretelling the future [prĭ-dĭk'-shən]

prescription: a written order for medicine [prĭ-skrĭp'-shən]

promotion: an advancement in rank or position [prə-mō'-shən]

reaction: a response [rē-ăk′-shən]

reconstruction: the act of putting back together [rē′-kən-strŭk′-shən]

regression: a movement backward to an earlier state [rĭ-grĕsh′-ən]

-ity state, quality, act
brevity: quality of being brief; shortness in time [brĕv-ĭ-tē]

equanimity: calm temperament, evenness of temper [ĕ′-kwə-nĭm′-ĭ-tē]

equity: fairness; the state of being just or fair [ĕk′-wĭ-tē]

il-ity state, quality, act
mobility: relating to the quality of being able to move [mō-bĭl′-i-tē]

-ive tending to or performing
disruptive: tending towards a break in the normal course or process [dĭs-rŭp′-tĭv]

at-ive tending to or performing
cumulative: gradually building up [kyōōm′-yə-lə′-tĭv]

-ize to make, to act
recognize: to identify someone or something seen before [rĕk′-əg-nīz′]

-ment that which
fragment: a broken piece [frăg′-mənt]

-ous having the quality of
carnivorous: flesh-eating [kär-nĭv′-ər-əs]

herbivorous: plant-eating [hûr-bĭv′-ər-əs]

luminous: giving off or reflecting light [lōō′-mə-nəs]

-tion state, quality, act
cognition: process of acquiring knowledge [kŏg-nĭsh′-ən]

i-tion state, quality, act
volition: the act of making a choice or decision [və-lĭsh′-ən]

-trix feminine
aviatrix: a woman airplane pilot [ā′-vē-ā′-trĭks]

-ulous having the quality of
incredulous: disbelieving; not believing [ĭn-krĕj′-ə-ləs]

-ure state, quality, act; that which; process, condition
fracture: a break, crack, or split [frăk′-chər]

infrastructure: underlying framework of a system [ĭn′-frə-strŭk′-chər]

recapture: the taking back of something [rē-kăp′-chər]

rupture: a breaking apart or the state of being broken apart [rŭp′-chər]

-y state, quality, act; body, group
memory: an ability to retain knowledge; an individual's stock of retained knowledge [mĕm′-ə-rē]

PRONUNCIATION KEY

ă	asp, fat, parrot		yōō	use, cute, few
ā	ape, date, play		yō	united, cure, globule
ä	ah, car, father		ûr	urn, fur, deter
ĕ	elf, ten, berry		ə	a in ago
ē	even, meet, money			e in agent
ĭ	is, hit, mirror			i in sanity
ī	ice, bite, high			o in comply
ō	open, tone, go			u in focus
ô	all, horn, law		ər	perhaps, murder
ōō	ooze, tool, crew		zh	azure, leisure
oo	look, pull, moor			

© 2012 The Critical Thinking Co.™ • www.CriticalThinking.com • 800-458-4849